Soccer School

Name: ..........................................

Class: ........................................

Coaches: ....................................

Kickito Ergo Sum

To Aldyr

A. B.

To ABC, with love

B. L.

For my mum

S. G.

Text copyright © 2018 by Alex Bellos and Ben Lyttleton
Illustrations copyright © 2018 by Spike Gerrell

First U.S. edition 2019

Library of Congress Catalog Card Number 2018961614
ISBN 978-1-5362-0695-1

19 20 21 22 23 24 LSC 10 9 8 7 6 5 4 3 2 1

Printed in Crawfordsville, IN, U.S.A.

This book was typeset in Palatino.
The illustrations were done in ink with digital manipulation.

Walker Books U.S.
a division of
Candlewick Press
99 Dover Street
Somerville, Massachusetts 02144

www.walkerbooksus.com

MIX
Paper from
responsible sources
FSC® C132124
www.fsc.org

# S⚽CCER SCHOOL

## season 3

### WHERE SOCCER ~~EXPLAINS~~ Tackles THE WORLD

### Alex Bellos & Ben Lyttleton

illustrated by Spike Gerrell

WALKER BOOKS

# MEET YOUR COACHES

## ALEX "BELLINHOS" BELLOS

66 Tudo bem, amigo? 99

## coach stats

Birthplace: Oxford, England
Birthday: November 22
Favorite food: Pickled gherkins
Favorite word: Four (because it's the only word that accurately describes the number of letters it has!)
Favorite ice-cream flavor: Chocolate
Favorite TV show: Any sports documentary
Favorite joke: Time flies like an arrow.
   Fruit flies like a banana.
Number of soccer balls in house: 3
Three favorite forwards: Pelé, Marta,
   Lionel Messi
Favorite stadium visited: San Siro, Milan
Favorite soccer trick: Seal dribble
Preferred goal celebration: Brazilian samba dance

☆☆☆ **coach** stats

Birthplace: London, England
Birthday: September 18
Favorite food: Pizza
Favorite word: GOAAAALLL!
Favorite ice-cream flavor: Honeycomb
Favorite TV show: Match of the Day
Favorite joke: Alex's hair (not really!)
Number of soccer balls in house: 7
Three favorite forwards: Kylian Mbappé, Johan Cruyff, Nadia Nadim
Favorite stadium visited: Estádio Municipal de Braga, Portugal
Favorite soccer trick: Rainbow flick
Preferred goal celebration: The airplane

BEN "THE PEN" LYTTLETON

66 Penalty, ref! 99

# CLASS SCHEDULE

|  | **MONDAY** | **TUESDAY** |
|---|---|---|
| **HOMEROOM** | | |
| **1st PERIOD** | **BIOLOGY** 1 | **ZOOLOGY** 36 |
| **2nd PERIOD** | | |
| **3rd PERIOD** | **ENGLISH** 10 | **POLITICAL SCIENCE** 50 |
| **4th PERIOD** | | |
| **LUNCH    1:00–2:00 PM** | | |
| **5th PERIOD** | **PHYSICS** 24 | **HEALTH** 62 |

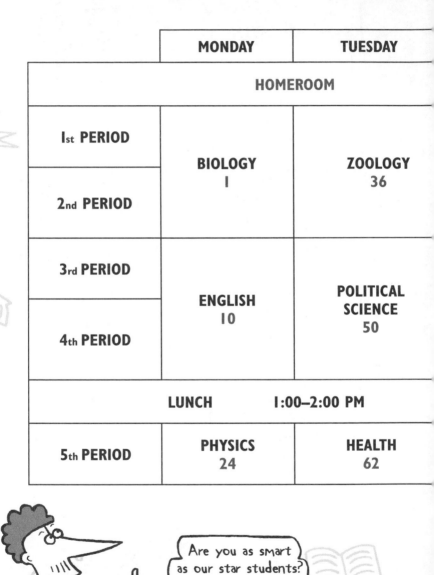

Are you as smart as our star students?

| WEDNESDAY | THURSDAY | FRIDAY |
|---|---|---|
| 8:30–8:40 AM | | |
| | HISTORY 86 | CHEMISTRY 124 |
| FIELD TRIP 74 | MATH 98 | FASHION 136 |
| | LUNCH | 1:00–2:00 PM |
| | GEOGRAPHY 112 | ENGINEERING 150 |

Find the answers to the quizzes on page 164. But no cheating!

E = MC²

Professional soccer players seem to glow. Their well-toned bodies and perfect posture are signs of fitness and well-being. They spend money on dentistry to make sure they have gleaming white teeth. Many male players feature a fashionable flourish of hair. Altogether, they are a sight to behold.

Just don't look at their feet!

Claw toes. Bruises. Blisters. Bunions. Calluses. Corns. Swelling. Plantar warts. Ewww! Soccer players' feet are victims of a lifetime of kicking a ball around for hours a day. And a lot can go wrong with a foot if it is not cared for properly. Believe us — we've spoken to an expert!

Look at my beautiful hair!

Claw blimey!

To kick off Season 3 at Soccer School, we are going to look at our lowermost limbs: those five-pronged platforms that often bear the weight of our entire body.

There's trouble afoot, and we're not going to tiptoe around the details!

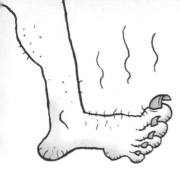

# POD SQUAD

A doctor who specializes in feet is called a **podiatrist**. Many teams employ a podiatrist because it is so important that players keep their feet in good condition. Just as firefighters take care of their hoses, singers take care of their voices, and our illustrator, Spike, takes care of his pencils, soccer players must look after their feet in order to do their jobs properly.

We spoke to Nutan Shah, one of the U.K.'s top podiatrists, who has worked with many top teams and the England national team. She's peeled the socks off the subject to let us know the ugly truth about soccer players' tootsies. "Not a pretty sight!" she revealed to us. "The feet get battered. A few players have immaculate feet but very few."

It pays to look after your paws. Shah says that a soccer player's most valuable accessories are not fancy sunglasses, a fast car, or the latest phone, but a pair of nail clippers and a nail file. Badly looked-after feet can mean players miss weeks of action.

Soccer players are all too aware of their disfigured trotters, which is why Shah told us that at the end of the season they often ask her if she can make their feet look pretty. "They are about to go on vacation, and they want their feet to look nice on the beach. Soccer players are able to look after their hands and face throughout the season, but their feet are completely bashed around."

# TIPS FOR TOES

When it comes to looking after your feet, the first thing to get right is the size of your shoes.

Soccer players often wear cleats that are too tight, maybe a size or a size and a half smaller than what their podiatrist recommends. Many players prefer tight cleats because they feel like a second skin, which gives more control of the ball. But it creates foot problems down the line. It's a pressing issue!

Soccer players also need to be very careful about the shoes they wear in their free time. Podiatrists see problems emerge when players wear stiff fashionable shoes that rub against their feet and give them calluses, blisters, and even open sores called ulcers. If an athlete wants to protect their Achilles tendons, they need to wear shoes that have a small incline in the heel, so flat shoes like sneakers and flip-flops are not recommended. Nor are stilettos!

Another major problem is moisture. This isn't just because soccer players run around a lot, which gives them hot and sweaty feet. It's also because

they spend so much time washing and soaking their feet in water. As part of their fitness and hygiene routines, soccer players are often in the shower, whirlpool, or bath. If their feet stay too wet, they are at risk of fungal infections, and if they dry out too much, they can get cracked skin. Sensible players will rub moisturizer on their feet. Smooth!

## Foot Complaints

**athlete's foot** • An itchy rash caused by a tiny fungus that eats dead skin. It got its name because the fungus thrives in moist, warm places like the damp surfaces in swimming pools and gyms, where athletes often spend their time. To avoid catching athlete's foot, it's advisable to wear flip-flops at the pool or gym.

Delicious dead skin!

**black toe** • If a player hits a toe hard — perhaps when they kick the ground by mistake or when another player steps on their foot — the skin underneath the nail can bleed, turning it black

or purple. In certain cases of black toe, the entire nail will eventually fall off.

**callus** • A yellowy blob of hard skin, usually caused by something hard rubbing against the skin continuously for a long time. For example, the little lump many people get on their middle finger from where a pencil rubs when they write is a callus. Calluses tend to appear on the feet more than anywhere else because whenever we walk or run, our feet rub against the inside of our shoes. A small callus can help protect the foot, but once it gets big, it causes discomfort and may have to be removed. Soccer players and other athletes are susceptible to calluses, especially if their cleats are too tight.

**claw toe** • A condition where all the toes, apart from the big toe, curl in, so that rather than lying flat, they look like animal claws. Most soccer players have claw toe, the result of wearing too-tight cleats from a young age. Players who have claw toe are 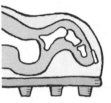 more likely to damage their toenails and get more calluses and corns.

**corn** • A hard, circular callus on the toe that is caused by friction on a single point. In some extreme cases, corns have to be filed down or sliced off with a knife.

**ingrown toenail** • When a toenail is not clipped properly, there is the risk that it may start to grow into the skin. Ingrown toenails are not a silly little problem. They can cause huge pain and easily lead to a soccer player having to take weeks off injured. To avoid them, players should check their toenails every day and file down any sharp bits that might dig into the skin.

**plantar wart** • A wart on the sole of the foot. Plantar warts are contagious and can be spread through communal showers and swimming pools. Soccer teams are obsessively vigilant about plantar warts, since they can quickly spread through an entire team. One treatment for a painful wart is to have a doctor freeze it so it falls off.

## Foot Anatomy

The **anatomy** of a living thing is its internal structure. Here's a glimpse into the anatomy of the foot — as you'll see, it's quite a *feet* of engineering!

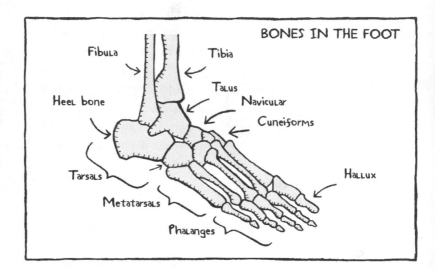

BONES IN THE FOOT

Fibula
Tibia
Talus
Heel bone
Navicular
Cuneiforms
Tarsals
Hallux
Metatarsals
Phalanges

**bones** • Each foot contains twenty-six bones and thirty-three joints, meaning that about a quarter of all the bones in our body are in the feet. The only limbs in our body with a more complicated bone structure are our hands, but for people who are ambulatory, feet undergo much more physical stress than hands because they carry the entire weight of the body. The bones that are the most at risk of injury for soccer players are the **metatarsals**, on the forefoot, since they are the thinnest bones in the foot and (unlike the **phalanges**, in the toes) cannot flex out of the way.

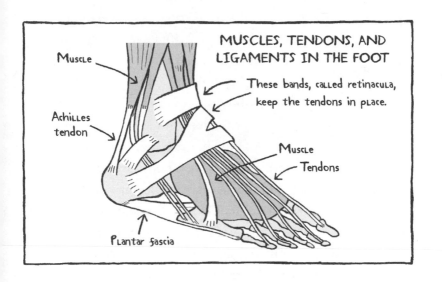

**MUSCLES, TENDONS, AND LIGAMENTS IN THE FOOT**

Muscle

Achilles tendon

These bands, called retinacula, keep the tendons in place.

Muscle

Tendons

Plantar fascia

**ligaments** • Ligaments join bones to bones. An important ligament in the foot is the **plantar fascia**, which runs along the sole from the heel to the toes. When you step on your foot, the plantar fascia stretches like a spring, and when you lift your foot up, the ligament releases, giving the foot a bounce of energy. It is literally a spring in your step!

**skin** • The skin under the ball of the foot and under the heel is thicker than the skin anywhere else on our body. This is because there are extra layers of fat, a bit like Bubble Wrap, which act as shock absorbers when we walk. Comfy!

**tendons** • Tendons join muscle to bone. The main tendon in the foot is the **Achilles tendon**, which joins the calf muscle to the heel. The Achilles tendon acts like a lever that pushes the foot away from the leg, which is what enables us to run, jump, walk up stairs, and stand on tiptoe. Scientists have discovered that sprinters, on average, have shorter Achilles tendons than other people — which gives them more force when pushing off the ground.

# FOOT FROMAGE

Everyone with a nose knows that feet often infuse socks with a distinctive cheesy aroma. You should smell Ben's after he's gone for a run! This pungent perfume is the result of the fact that the soles of the feet (along with the palms of the hands) have the highest density of sweat glands in the human body. Sweat on its own does not smell, but moist, warm socks provide the perfect habitat for **bacteria** that live on the skin to thrive. The bacteria eat dead skin, and the process produces a smelly gas with a familiar cheesy scent. Scientists who study smelly socks discovered that the same malodorous bacteria in our feet are present in smelly cheeses, such as Limburger, from Germany. Pee-yew!

TONY HEALEY

★ STAR STUDENT

66 Best foot forward! 99

☆☆☆ STAR STUDENT   Stats

Toes: 10
Black toes: 9
Pairs of high-heeled shoes: 0
Bottles of moisturizer: 6
Birthplace: Seoul, South Korea
Supports: Achilles '29 (Netherlands)
Fave player: Steve Archibald
Trick: Scores toe-poke goals from outside area

# BIOLOGY QUIZ

1. **What is the name of a doctor who specializes in treating feet?**

   a) Podiatrist
   b) Sole man
   c) Faith heeler
   d) Head, shoulders, knees, and toes surgeon

2. **Former England striker Darius Vassell once missed three games due to injury because he did what to his toe after it had become swollen?**

   a) He tried to clip off the nail but cut a chunk out of his toe.
   b) He peeled off the toenail by accident, and it became too painful to put his cleats on.
   c) He drilled through his nail to drain the blood and ease the pressure, and the toe became infected.
   d) He painted the toenail with nail polish and became ill from inhaling the fumes.

3. **How did Achilles, the hero from Greek mythology for whom the tendon in our heel is named, die?**

   a) A lightning bolt hit him on the heel.
   b) A poisoned arrow hit him on the heel.
   c) A snake bit him on the heel.
   d) A soccer ball hit him on the heel.

4. **Which of the following players has the biggest feet?**

   a) Cristiano Ronaldo
   b) David Silva
   c) Paul Pogba
   d) Romelu Lukaku

5. **Which animal is attracted to the smell of sweaty socks?**

   a) Tiger
   b) Skunk
   c) Mosquito
   d) Snail

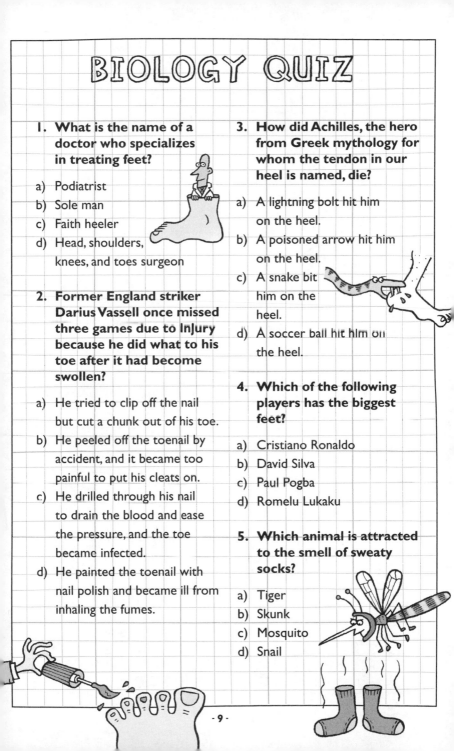

Listen up! Do you like the sound of your own voice? Do you get in trouble for talking too much? Do you love words—and soccer? Would you like to talk about soccer for the rest of your life? Well, we might have the job for you! You'd have to travel a lot and

have the gift of gab, but you'd also get to watch all the drama of the biggest games unfold live in front of you. Too exciting for words!

In this lesson, we are going to learn the secrets of TV soccer commentary. Commentators describe the action and provide information during games to make them more enjoyable for viewers watching at home. We'll see how they use colorful and creative language to maximum effect.

This is one lesson where you do need to talk in class. Speak up!

# TRICKS OF THE TRADE

If you want to be a TV commentator, the following tips for your tongue should be on the tip of your tongue! At Soccer School, we call this the Guide for Orally Astonishing Language Skills, or GOALS.

## 1. LOVE YOUR LARYNX

Just as soccer players ensure that their bodies are in top condition before a game, commentators need to make sure that their voices are well cared for. If it is cold, wear a scarf. Avoid smoky places, since this will protect your throat. Also, avoid shouting or whispering, since you don't want to strain your vocal cords in the run-up to the game.

## 2. DANNY, DRINK WATER!

Talking for ninety minutes at a time is tough on your throat, and you don't want it to dry out. No croaking, please! To make sure your throat is well hydrated before the game, take small sips of water throughout the day and eat foods such as cucumbers, tomatoes, spinach, and watermelon, which are full of water. Don't eat spicy foods, as they can irritate your throat. But don't drink too much — you don't have time to go to the bathroom mid-game!

## 3. PREP YOUR PENCIL CASE

This is one job where you need to bring a pencil case to work! Commentators use different colored pens and highlighters to make notes on the team sheets.

# 4. STUDY THE TEAMS

Write up a crib sheet for both teams on a single piece of paper. Put the players' names and numbers in their correct positions, and for each player, add a relevant fact, as we've done below. (We did just one team, but you will need to do both). Memorize the players' names and numbers. Look to see if any facts jump out.

DATE: Today

TEAM NAME: Commentary City

**11**
**Diego Gonzalez**
First Venezuelan
in the league

**9**
**Harry Dane**
29 goals so far
(2 hat tricks,
5 headers)

**10**
**Charlie Crosser**
12 assists, all
with right foot

**7**
**Lionel Tidy**
Made Argentina
debut last week

**4**
**Edgar N. Forcer**
First game after
6-month knee injury

**8**
**Davie Disco**
Scored 8 free kicks
this season

**3**
**Junior Tackles**
Debut game,
only 17

**5**
**Bertie Boxer**
Birthday today,
turning 24

**6**
**Cruncher Bones**
5 red cards

**2**
**Philip Fitness**
Played every
minute
last game

**1**
**Gary Gloves**
Saved 3 penalties

# 5. PRACTICE PRONUNCIATION

James . . . Hamms . . . Yah Mez . . . Hames . . . Ja Mezz

James Rodríguez

Players come from all over the world, and their names are not always easy to pronounce. Because different languages pronounce the same letters in different ways, it's always worth asking someone from a player's country of origin for the correct pronunciation. Here is our list of five soccer players whose names might get a commentator's tongue in a twist:

| NAME | NATIONALITY | PRONUNCIATION |
|---|---|---|
| James Rodríguez | Colombian | HAH-mess rod-REE-gess |
| César Azpilicueta | Spanish | SAY-zar ath-PEE-lee-koo-et-ah |
| Gonzalo Higuaín | Argentinian | goh-ZAH-lo ee-gwah-YEEN |
| İlkay Gündoğan | German | ILK-eye GUN-doe-wan |
| Toby Alderweireld | Belgian | TOE-bee AL-der-vay-reld |

# 6. THINK ABOUT THE STORY

Consider the circumstances leading up to the game. What are fans interested in? Is it the World Cup final, a derby game between two local rivals, or is one of the coaches under pressure after a string of poor results? You need to have a firm grasp of the game's backstory, because at the final whistle, the fans don't just want to know the score—they want to know what the result means for them: *United wins the European Cup! Rovers are relegated to a lower division! The coach could now lose his job!*

# 7. PUT THE KETTLE ON

The game is about to start. You have your pens, the team sheet . . . all you need now is a cup of tea! Make yourself an herbal tea with honey and lemon, which will help soothe your throat once those vocal cords spring into action. Beware of drinking fizzy drinks while commentating, since they will put air in your stomach. You don't want to burp on live TV!

# 8. BE ENTHUSIASTIC (WITHIN REASON!)

To be a good commentator, you not only need to be interested in soccer—you also need to *sound* interested in soccer. Your voice must be positive and enthusiastic. Do-not-speak-with-no-e-mo-tion-like-a-ro-bot. But don't get too excited! DON'T SHOUT! Don't start off too enthusiastic, because then how can you turn up the excitement when there is something really dramatic, like a goal or a red card? We recommend starting at about 60 percent volume, so you can scale it up to 100 percent when a goal is scored. But don't get too caught up in the excitement—you need to remember to breathe!

Not everyone gets it right the first time. Hundreds of viewers complained when former England player Phil Neville commentated his first game during the 2014 World Cup. They said he was boring! But he practiced and improved.

In club soccer, fans of both teams may be watching, so try not to favor one team over the other: regardless of the team you support, you must stay impartial. For international soccer, the rules are a bit different. If, say, England is playing another country, then the commentators for English TV will tend to favor England, because most of the viewers will be England supporters.

## 9. DON'T, UMM, HESITATE

Be confident with what you say and what you don't. Try not to use filler words, such as "umm," "uhh," or "like" in the middle of a sentence. These words mean nothing and get in the way of what you are trying to say. Here are a few techniques to avoid falling flat with fillers:

**RELAX:** The more anxious you are, the more likely you are to use a filler word.

**SLOW DOWN:** If you speak slowly, you won't get tongue-tied and forget what you're saying.

**PAUSE:** Wait at the end of a sentence before starting a new one. It can add impact to your words and create a rhythm to your speech.

**LISTEN:** Record yourself speaking to hear if and when you use filler words.

## 10. NAME THE PLAYERS

When a player does something important, like score a goal, you need to identify that player right away. It's not always easy! The action can be very fast, and sometimes you can't see the player's number. Use other clues to recognize a player, such as position, tattoos, running style, or even their haircut. But be careful: some players might change their hairstyle just before a game!

In 1942 in Brazil, one nearsighted commentator had a trick to make sure that he knew who the goal scorer was. He yelled "Gooooooaaaal" for as long as possible, which gave enough time for his sidekick to write down the player's name on a piece of paper for him to read. The phrase "Gooooooaaaal" caught on and is now used by commentators in numerous countries.

## 11. ENJOY THE SILENCE

Radio commentary is different from TV commentary. On the radio, you need to talk all the time, because if there is silence, listeners might think the radio has broken! TV viewers know that the TV hasn't broken because they can see the picture. So on TV, if there is a quiet moment in the game without much action, you don't need to describe it. You can keep silent for a few seconds, but stay on the ball!

## 12. ENHANCE THE PICTURES

The job of a TV commentator is to add to what the audience is already seeing. For example, if Luis Suárez passes the ball to Lionel Messi, you don't say, "Luis Suárez passes the

ball to Lionel Messi," because everyone watching can see that! However, saying "Messi makes an intelligent run into space to receive Suárez's pass" gives additional information that helps the viewer understand the game in greater detail.

## 13. OH, MY WORDS!

It's boring to listen to words that are repeated too often. Developing a wide range of available words, or **vocabulary**, will ensure that you always have a new one handy. The best way to build your vocabulary is to read—and not just the Soccer School books! Any book or magazine will give you access to new words, and that's the best way for your brain to take them on board. One soccer writer calculated there are seventy-three different ways to describe how a goal is scored! Here are just a few:

ARROWED

CURLED

FIRED

SCRAMBLED

HOOKED

SLOTTED

Can you think of any more?

Now think of different ways you can describe a header that leads to a goal: Crashing! Glancing! Towering! Angled! Diving!

As you can tell, we love words around here!

Commentators also use language creatively. For example, they use **metaphor** and **simile**. A metaphor is a word or phrase that we use to describe something as if it were something else, so that it paints a picture of what's going on. When a commentator says that the Wembley Stadium field is a green carpet, they don't mean that it's an actual carpet! They mean that it is neat, tidy, and luxuriant, like a brand-new carpet. When they say that the game is on a knife-edge, they do not mean that the game is literally on a knife blade; they mean that it is dangerously balanced, as if on the thin edge of a knife.

A simile is when we compare one thing with another using the word *like* or *as*. Like metaphors, similes help make descriptions vivid. Examples might include "Alex leaped like a salmon to head it home" or "Ben dribbled past his markers as quickly as an Olympic skier."

The best commentators use metaphors and similes all the time. Listen hard and see how many you can catch.

# 14. BE NATURAL

Commentators need to be able to think on the spot. If a good idea comes to you during the game, write it down. Ben's friend Dave commentated when Greece knocked out France at Euro 2004. Just before the end of the game, he thought of a joke based on the name of France's former emperor Napoléon Bonaparte. He used it on the final whistle: "Napoléon Blown Apart! France is out of the competition!" A joke that is a play on words is called a **pun**. At Soccer School, we love puns!

If you get the giggles or need to cough while commentating, it's not the end of the world. Professionals do that too. One TV commentator told us: "When I have a laughing fit, I prefer to go with it and I just hope the viewers join in!" So go ahead . . . LOL!

# CLUELESS COMMENTATORS

Some commentators are remembered for saying silly things. Here are some examples of who said what, and why it was wrong:

## TAUTOLOGY

When you say the same thing twice in different words.

> If that had gone in, it would have been a goal!

David Coleman

> Soccer's soccer. If that weren't the case, it wouldn't be the game that it is.

Garth Crooks

## CONTRADICTION

When you say two things that are the opposite of each other.

> Brazil is totally reliant on one player—Neymar at one end and Thiago Silva at the other.

Martin Keown

> They're the second-best team in the world, and there's no higher praise than that.

Kevin Keegan

## MALAPROPISM

When you use the wrong word in the place of a similar-sounding one.

Newcastle is absolutely besotted by injuries.

Mark Lawrenson

Costa is the vital cog in the Chelsea jigsaw.

Jamie Redknapp

LARRY LARYNX

☆ STAR STUDENT

Soccer School

"Shout it out!"

☆☆☆ STAR STUDENT Stats

Ums and uhhs: 0
Highlighter pens: 7
Throat drops: 12
Longest "Gooooaaal": 36 seconds
Birthplace: Chattanooga, TN
Supports: Llanfairpwllgwyngyll-gogerychwyrndrobwllllantysilio-gogogoch FC (Wales)
Fave player: Michael Tonge
Trick: Commentating on his own
☆ goals

# ENGLISH QUIZ

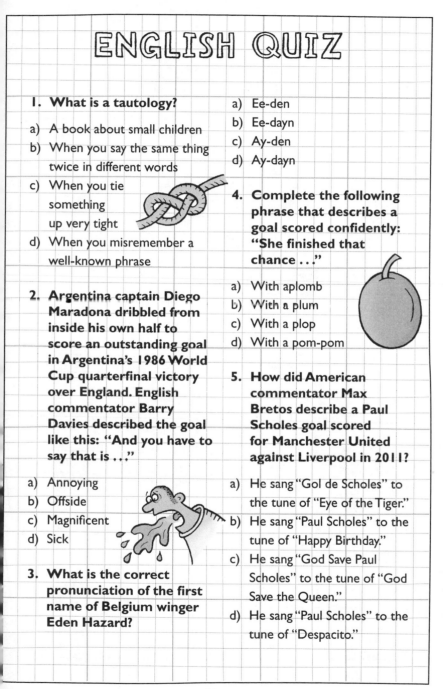

**1. What is a tautology?**

a) A book about small children
b) When you say the same thing twice in different words
c) When you tie something up very tight
d) When you misremember a well-known phrase

**2. Argentina captain Diego Maradona dribbled from inside his own half to score an outstanding goal in Argentina's 1986 World Cup quarterfinal victory over England. English commentator Barry Davies described the goal like this: "And you have to say that is ..."**

a) Annoying
b) Offside
c) Magnificent
d) Sick

**3. What is the correct pronunciation of the first name of Belgium winger Eden Hazard?**

a) Ee-den
b) Ee-dayn
c) Ay-den
d) Ay-dayn

**4. Complete the following phrase that describes a goal scored confidently: "She finished that chance ..."**

a) With aplomb
b) With a plum
c) With a plop
d) With a pom-pom

**5. How did American commentator Max Bretos describe a Paul Scholes goal scored for Manchester United against Liverpool in 2011?**

a) He sang "Gol de Scholes" to the tune of "Eye of the Tiger."
b) He sang "Paul Scholes" to the tune of "Happy Birthday."
c) He sang "God Save Paul Scholes" to the tune of "God Save the Queen."
d) He sang "Paul Scholes" to the tune of "Despacito."

# PHYSICS

Professional soccer players come in all sizes. Some players are short and others are tall. Just like your coaches at Soccer School! Alex is shorter than Ben, although he grows a little taller when his hair gets super curly.

This lesson is about height. On the field, being tall is an advantage in some situations; in others, being short is better. We are going to learn about how our ability to run and dribble changes depending on our feet . . . and our height!

We will also meet a world-famous soccer player who feared he was too small to make it, and we'll learn the tallest and shortest nationalities in the world. That's the long and short of it. Now, let's aim high!

# THE BOY WHO WOULD NOT GROW

Messi before ↓

Lionel Messi is one of the world's greatest-ever soccer players. Many people think the Argentinean forward is the best player in the history of the game. But when he was younger, Messi had a medical condition and was worried that he might be too short to become a professional player. He also suffered at the hands of bullies who were mean about his height. His story can tell us a lot about the dedication and sacrifice he made at a young age to fulfill his dreams. And of course it shows us that great things can come in small packages!

Messi grew up in Rosário, a city in Argentina. He joined local team Newell's Old Boys when he was just six years old. His youth team won almost every game they played in. But by the time Messi was ten, all his teammates were growing taller much faster than he was.

When Messi failed to have a growth spurt, he visited Dr. Diego Schwarzstein. The doctor discovered that Messi had a rare growth **hormone** disorder. Hormones are chemicals produced by our body that control how our body and emotions work. It turned out that Messi's **pituitary gland**, a pea-size organ in the brain responsible for the balance of hormones, was not sending out the right amount of growth hormone. A lack of this hormone can lead to poor vision and lowered immunity—issues that could have prevented Messi from turning professional. The doctor prescribed Messi with a three-year course of treatment.

It was a tough time. "Every night, I had to stick a needle into my legs, night after night after night, every day of the week, and this over a period of three years," Messi said.

In the middle of Messi's course of treatment, Argentina suffered a financial crisis, and Messi's family was no longer able to pay for the growth hormones. The treatment was expensive, costing around $1,000 per month. Newell's Old Boys could not afford it, nor could River Plate, another team that was interested in Messi. Only one team was prepared to sign Messi and take on the costs of the treatment for another year. That team was Barcelona. So at the age of just thirteen, he moved to a new country with his father, Jorge.

Messi went on to make Barcelona the greatest team of his generation. He has won more than eight league titles, four Champions Leagues, and three Club World Cup titles with Barcelona, and he has won the Ballon D'Or award for the world's best player five times. If you put all his trophies on top of one another, they would be taller than he is!

Messi is now 5 feet 7 inches/1.70 meters and taller than Diego Maradona, Argentina's former World Cup–winning captain. "I don't know if you will be better than Maradona, but you will be taller," Dr. Schwarzstein had promised him. At Soccer School, we believe you should never give up on your dreams—and Messi has definitely reached the very top!

Messi after

# HOW MESSI HIT THE HEIGHTS

Messi, who is one of the best dribblers in the history of the game, is shorter than the average soccer player. His small stature is not unusual for those with dribbling skills: many of the best dribblers in the game are short.

**FIVE BEST SHORT DRIBBLERS**

Fran Kirby (England) 5 ft. 2 in./1.57 m
Jimmy Johnstone (Scotland) 5 ft. 2 in./1.57 m
Diego Maradona (Argentina) 5 ft. 5 in./1.65 m
Raheem Sterling (England) 5 ft. 6 in./1.68 m
Lionel Messi (Argentina) 5 ft. 7 in./1.70 m

Short people make better dribblers than tall people because short people find it easier to control their balance when running with the ball than tall people do. Tallies are more likely to topple, but shorties will usually stay up!

To understand why short people can control their balance better, we need to learn about the laws of **physics**. Physics is the study of how everything moves around the universe. And when we say everything, we mean EVERYTHING. Physicists are interested in the movement of big things like planets, small things like atoms . . . and medium-size things like soccer players.

## A-MASS-ING

**Mass** is the amount of stuff in an object. An object's center of mass, or center of gravity, is a point usually in the middle of that object. The object balances around this point.

CENTER OF MASS

The center of mass of a human standing up is in the middle of the body, somewhere around the height of the belly button. If our center of mass is directly above our feet and legs, as it is when we are standing up straight, then we are stable and will not fall over.

But if our center of mass is not directly above our legs and feet, such as when we are pushed, we are unstable and will fall over unless we move our center of mass back between our legs and feet. We can return to stability by standing straight again, or by placing our legs farther apart.

Now let's think about what a player is doing when dribbling the ball. The player is constantly darting from side to side, speeding up and then slowing down. Their center of mass is moving all over the place, going from positions that are stable to positions that are unstable and back again.

- 29 -

# SHORT AND STEADY

A short player has shorter, lighter limbs and so in general will find it easier to control their center of mass than a tall player. For example, if a short player and a tall player lean forward at the same angle, all other things being equal, the tall player will actually be leaning farther than the short player, because the tall player has a longer body. This means that tall players are more likely to topple and have to use more energy to steady themselves. Small players spend less energy on maintaining stability, which means they can spend more energy on running, speeding up, and controlling the ball.

If you look at how a tall player like Cristiano Ronaldo dribbles, you'll see he uses tiny steps. If he made big steps, he would be wasting lots of energy moving his large, heavy bones around to make sure he is stable. But a much shorter (and lighter) player, like Lionel Messi, dribbles using small steps or big steps—which is one of the reasons Messi is so hard to defend against. You never know which way he will go!

## TALL ORDER

We've seen how shortness can be an advantage for dribblers. Now let's look at a position where tall is usually best: wearers of the number 1 shirt. Because goalkeepers can use their hands, tall ones can usually reach higher to catch crosses that are intended for strikers.

But it is more than just feet and inches. Scientists have shown that taller people are better at judging distances, so they can more accurately identify the position of the ball. This may be because they are used to looking at the ground from farther away.

# HEIGHTOMETER

Scientists looked at the height of more than thirty thousand professional male players from thirty-one European countries to calculate the average height of players by position:

Goalkeepers: 6'2"/**1.89** m

Defenders: 6'0"/**1.83** m

Midfielders: 5'10½"/**1.79** m

Forwards: 5'11½"/**1.82** m

## LOOKING HIGH AND LOW

Soccer has a huge variety of heights among its players. Some sports are better suited to tall athletes, while others are best for smaller athletes:

| SPORT | AVERAGE HEIGHT |
|---|---|
| Basketball | 6 ft. 7 in./2.00 m |
| Volleyball | 6 ft. 7 in./2.00 m |
| Football | 6 ft. 3 in./1.91 m |
| Ski jumping | 5 ft. 9 in./1.75 m |
| Gymnastics | 5 ft. 4 in./1.63 m |

## TAKING THE HIGH ROAD

Tottenham Hotspur's 9–1 Premier League win over Wigan in 2009 broke goal-scoring records, but it also made history for a height-related reason. Peter Crouch, one of the Premier League's tallest players at 6 feet 7 inches/2.01 meters, opened the scoring. Aaron Lennon, who is 5 feet 5 inches/1.65 meters, scored the fifth goal for the Spurs: the teammates' height difference of 14 inches/36 centimeters is the biggest in Premier League history!

# HEADS YOU WIN!

Tim Cahill is one of the best headers in the history of soccer. The Australia midfielder is 5 feet 10 inches / 1.78 meters tall, which makes him much shorter than most of the defenders he plays against. "I head a ball like someone else kicks it," he said. But how? First, he works hard in the gym, building power in his legs to give added spring to help him launch into the air, and building upper body strength to keep defenders at bay. To get to the ball before taller defenders, he has to arrive in the right area at the perfect time. He puts out his arms as an elevation tool to propel him upward and uses his neck muscles to direct the ball. Also, he is fearless when he jumps for the ball, and he offers this advice to all future goal-getters: "Believe in your ability and place the ball out of the goalkeeper's reach."

Powerful neck muscles

Upper-body strength

Propel with arms

Fearless jumping

Strong Legs

Great timing

# HIGH

Here is where you will find the tallest, and the shortest, people in the world:

| TALLEST WOMEN | SHORTEST WOMEN | TALLEST MEN | SHORTEST MEN |
|---|---|---|---|
| Latvia | Guatemala | Netherlands | Timor-Leste |
| Netherlands | Philippines | Belgium | Yemen |
| Estonia | Bangladesh | Estonia | Laos PDR |
| Czech Republic | Nepal | Latvia | Madagascar |
| Serbia | Timor-Leste | Denmark | Malawi |

MINNIE SKULE

☆ STAR STUDENT

"High five!"

☆☆☆ STAR STUDENT Stats

Height: 4'10"/1.47 m
Dribbles per game: 54
Headed goals scored: 0
Friends who are gymnasts: 12
Birthplace: Tallahassee, FL
Supports: Talleres (Argentina)
Fave player: Emmanuel Petit
Trick: Wobbles but never falls

# PHYSICS QUIZ

1. **What is the name for the point in an object around which it balances?**

a) Center of mass
b) Center of math
c) Center of gravy
d) Balance point

2. **Which diminutive Brazilian legend was affectionately known by his fans as "Shorty"?**

a) Pelé
b) Ronaldo
c) Romário
d) Ronaldinho

3. **The pituitary gland controls our growth hormones, but where in the body is it?**

a) Under the arm
b) In the brain
c) At the back of the throat
d) In the heel

4. **What did a Dutch psychologist who studied the height of soccer referees discover?**

a) There are more goals with shorter referees.
b) There are more penalties with taller referees.
c) Shorter referees control games better.
d) Taller referees control games better.

5. **Kristof Van Hout, a goalkeeper from Belgium, is thought to be the tallest professional soccer player in the world. How tall is he?**

a) 6 ft. 10 in./2.08 m
b) 6 ft. 11 in./2.11 m
c) 7 ft./2.13 m
d) 7 ft. 1 in./2.16 m

$\mathbb{G}$o, Lions! Go, Elephants! Go, Leopards!

   No, we're not watching a wildlife documentary. We're cheering on some of our favorite African teams.

   Soccer is the most popular sport in Africa, a continent made up of fifty-four countries and with a population of 1.2 billion people. Africans like Mo Salah of Egypt and Victor Moses of Nigeria are among the world's best players.

   The national soccer teams of many African countries show their love for their continent's amazing wildlife by giving themselves animal nicknames. For example, Nigeria's team is known as the Super Eagles, Cameroon's is the Indomitable Lions, and Ivory Coast's is the Elephants.

   These animals are powerful symbols. Eagles fly high and swoop fast, lions prowl and devour their prey, and elephants are the biggest land animal on the planet. Yet not every country has chosen a well-known animal for its team nickname. The continent is home to thousands of species of mammals, fish, and birds, so there are some amazing animals to choose from.

   In this lesson, we're going to discover some of the surprising animals that are the nicknames for African national teams. *Tweet! Bleat! Hiss!*

# ON THE WING

**Country:** Uganda

**Nickname:** The Cranes

**Why?** The gray-crowned crane is the national bird of Uganda, appearing on its flag and coat of arms.

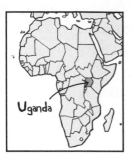

**What are they?** Cranes are tall birds, standing about 3 feet/1 meter high, with long legs and a long neck. In fact, the mechanical cranes you see on construction sites are named after these birds because of their long neck. There are fifteen species of cranes across the world, of which the gray-crowned crane is one. Its wingspan is huge—up to 6½ feet/2 meters, as wide as the exceedingly tall soccer player Peter Crouch is high. Gray-crowned cranes live in grasslands and wetlands in eastern and southern Africa.

**Distinguishing features:**
The gray-crowned crane has one of the best haircuts in the animal kingdom: a gold crown that looks like a bleached and crimped perm, not unlike the hairstyle many soccer players wore in the 1980s.

**Animal behavior:** Cranes are famous for their elaborate dance routines, which they use to attract mates. These routines include bobbing their head, fluttering their wings, twirling, jumping, bowing, and running. When humans sing songs near them, cranes get into the groove by nodding their head.

**Clever birds:** If a group of cranes is attacked by a predator, sometimes an adult crane will pretend it has an injury by limping in an exaggerated way so that the predator becomes interested in it, rather than the younger and more vulnerable chicks.

**Would cranes be any good at soccer?** Their long neck would make them good at heading. And their love of dance means they would have amazing goal celebrations. But they would risk getting into trouble with refs for fake injuries.

KEEP CALM AND CARRION

Many African national teams use birds as their nickname. Apart from the crane, parrot, and swallow, almost all are fierce birds of prey. These birds hunt and eat carrion (rotting dead animals). Feeling peckish, anyone?

Burundi: The Swallows
Mali: The Eagles
Sudan: The Jediane Falcons
Togo: The Sparrowhawks
Nigeria (men): The Super Eagles
Nigeria (women): The Super Falcons
Tunisia: The Eagles of Carthage
São Tomé and Príncipe: The Falcons and Parrots

# HOOF IT UP

**Country:** Ethiopia

**Nickname:** The Walias

**Why?** The name comes from the walia ibex, which is a rare species of wild goat that lives only in Ethiopia.

Ethiopia

**What are they?** The domestic goat we see on farms is actually one of only eight species of goats found around the world. Five of these goat species are mountain goats called ibexes. The walia ibex is the most endangered ibex species, with only about five hundred animals left in the wild. Their population was much larger, but they were killed by humans for their meat and fur. They are now found only in a small area of steep, jagged cliffs in Ethiopia's mountains, about 8,202 feet/2,500 meters high, where it is hard for humans to capture them.

**Distinguishing features:** Male walia ibexes are about 4½ feet/1.4 meters tall and have a light-brown coat and a white belly. They also have enormous curved horns, which can sometimes be more than 3 feet/1 meter in length. Old males have a thick black beard. The females are a lighter color and a bit smaller, with thinner horns.

**Animal behavior:** Ibexes are fantastic jumpers. They have to be, since they spend their days jumping up and down sheer cliff faces looking for plants to eat. An ibex can jump about 6½ feet / 2 meters high without a running start.

**Smart footwear:** An ibex hoof is the best climbing shoe in the animal kingdom. It is made up of two thin toes, each with a sharp, jagged edge that is perfect for clinging on to tiny footholds on steep and rocky cliffs. A soft, textured underside presses against the rock to give extra grip.

**Would walia ibexes be any good at soccer?** They would be amazing at jumping for corners, although they would need to be careful not to puncture the ball with their horns. The sturdy grip of their hooves means they would never skid in the rain, but they might be more interested in climbing the stands than staying on the field.

PARKING ZEBUS
The ibex is a bovid, the family of hoofed, horned, grass-eating mammals that includes sheep, cattle, goats, buffalo, bison, and antelopes. The munch bunch! Other African teams with bovid nicknames include:

Angola: The Sable Antelopes
Madagascar: The Barea (a species of zebu)
Niger: The Dama Gazelles

# VENOM-ENAL

**Country:** Mozambique

**Nickname:** The Mambas

**Why?** Mambas are venomous snakes, meaning that they will bite attackers and inject **venom**, or poison, into them. Two of the four species of mambas live in Mozambique, including the black mamba, which is one of the most feared snakes in the world.

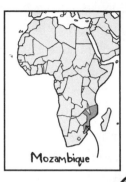

Mozambique

**What are they?** Black mambas are the longest snakes in Africa. Their average length is about 6½ feet / 2 meters, but they can grow to longer than 13 feet / 4 meters. Despite their name, they aren't actually black but various shades of brown and gray.

**Distinguishing features:** The tongue and insides of a mamba's mouth are completely black, as if it has been sucking an ink-flavored lollipop. When threatened, it will open its mouth, revealing the black inside. This defensive posture is a warning that the mamba might bite. You don't want to be bitten by a black mamba! A few drops of its venom will kill you, sometimes in only half an hour.

**Animal behavior:** The black mamba is the world's fastest snake. It can slither at around 12 miles/19 kilometers per hour, a speed at which most humans can run for only a short time. While it zooms along, it holds its head up 3 feet/1 meter in the air, which adds to its menacing appearance.

**Fearsome reputation:** Mambas are feared throughout Africa and feature in many stories and myths. But even though they are deadly enough to kill a human, they are generally shy creatures who avoid threats.

**Would mambas be any good at soccer?** The snakes would be super speedy running up the wing and good at slithering past defenders. The opposing team would run away in fear of being bitten. But not having any feet would be a big barrier to soccer success.

INSECT-A-SIDE
In addition to snakes, other venomous animals include spiders, bees, and jellyfish. These two African national teams have chosen venomous nicknames. They certainly have sting!

Gambia: The Scorpions
Rwanda: The Wasps

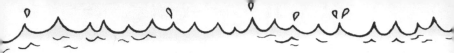

# GILL-INGHAM FC

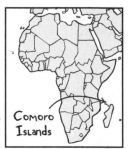

Comoro Islands

**Country:** Comoro Islands (or Comoros)

**Nickname:** The Coelacanths

**Why?** The coelacanth (pronounced SEE-luh-kanth) is a fish that lives in the ocean around the Comoro Islands, which are between Madagascar and the African mainland.

**What are they?** Coelacanths are one of the world's most fascinating fish. They are huge, up to 6½ feet / 2 meters long and weigh about 200 pounds / 89 kilograms. They are also famously ugly.

**Distinguishing features:** The coelacanth has been around since well before dinosaurs, making it one of the world's oldest species of fish. They were first discovered as fossils. Scientists assumed that the fish had become extinct millions of years ago, until one was discovered in 1938. Only about five hundred of them are believed to still be in existence, making them one of the rarest fish in the world.

**Animal behavior:** Coelacanths have a unique set of four finlike limbs that move in a pattern similar to the legs of a trotting horse. The coelacanth helps us understand **evolution**, which is the process in which life-forms slowly change their characteristics over millions of years. For example, hundreds of millions of years ago, there were fish in the sea but no animals living on land. Gradually, some fish evolved and emerged from the water to become land animals. Some scientists believe that these first land animals evolved from fish like the coelacanth.

**Fish-brained?** The coelacanth brain is tiny, taking up only about 1.5 percent of the space inside its skull. The skull also has a special hinge so that when a coelacanth opens its mouth wide—to eat big fish—its skull splits in two.

**Would coelacanths be any good at soccer?** Their limb-like fins would make them great underwater kickers, and their huge size and ugly appearance would intimidate opponents. But with its tiny brain and wide mouth, it might eat the ball (and the other players).

TEAMS WITH TEETH

The coelacanth has sharp teeth to help it catch its dinner, but its gnashers are not the most feared in African waters. These two African teams have chosen aquatic predators as their nicknames. They have bite!

Cape Verde: The Blue Sharks
Lesotho: The Crocodiles

# MAMMAL MIA!

Mammals are a type of animal that is warm-blooded, has a backbone, and has either fur or hair, like cats, dogs . . . and humans! Most of Africa's best-loved animals are mammals, like these:

## BIG CATS

The lion is the largest of the big cats in Africa and a symbol of strength and power around the world. It is therefore an obvious choice for a team nickname. Cameroon's national team is called the Indomitable Lions. Senegal's is called the Teranga Lions. (The word *teranga* means "hospitality" in Senegal's Wolof language and reflects the country's pride in being welcoming and generous to visitors.) Morocco's team is called the Atlas Lions, referring to a subspecies of lion from the Atlas Mountains, although none has lived in the wild there for almost a hundred years.

## LITTLE FOXES

The fennec fox is a tiny animal, even smaller than the domestic cat, but that didn't stop Algeria, one of the most successful teams in Africa, from choosing it as their nickname. The habitat of the fennec fox is the Sahara Desert, so it has to be tough to survive in extreme conditions. The fox's distinguishing feature is its jumbo-size ears, which help keep it cool by getting rid of excess heat.

## TINY RODENTS

But the smallest of all the mammals used as a nickname was chosen by Benin and is . . . the squirrel! The first president of Benin's soccer federation suggested the name in the 1960s because the squirrel is a plucky little thing that can climb high. However, many people in Benin feel that the team would perform better if it were named after a more aggressive, stronger animal, since bushy-tailed squirrels are unlikely to strike fear into the hearts of opponents. The sports minister has suggested the Emerging Panthers, and another suggestion was the Bees of Benin. *Buzz buzz!*

## DEAD AS A DODO

An animal is considered **endangered** if there are so few of them left that it is likely they will all die out. An **extinct** animal has died out. In the last five hundred years, at least 250 species of animals have become extinct. The most famous of them, the dodo, lived on the island of Mauritius. This tubby bird with a long beak died out because humans destroyed its habitat and also killed it for food.

The Mauritius national team is nicknamed the Dodos, but this isn't because good soccer players are an endangered species there, or possibly even extinct! The dodo is now a national symbol for the island, a reminder that animals can die out if we don't protect them.

FLORA N. FAUNA

★ STAR STUDENT

66 Wild about soccer! 99

★ STAR STUDENT Stats

Pet elephants: 10
Pet birds: 83
Pet ibexes: 22
Pet dodos: 0
Birthplace: Canary Islands, Spain
Supports: Wolves (U.K.)
Fave player: Danny Fox
Trick: Flying through the air to win headers

# ZOOLOGY QUIZ

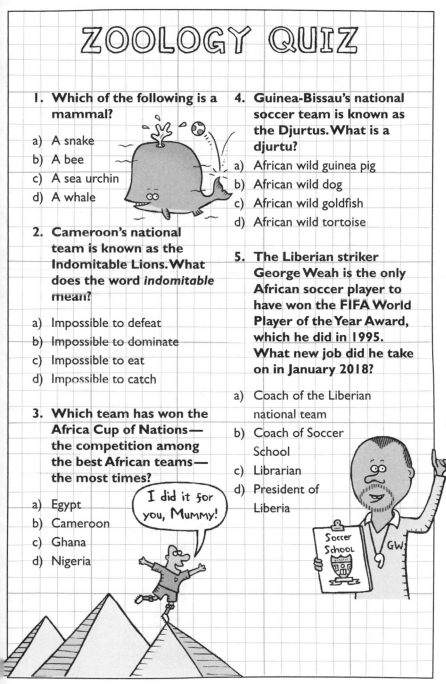

1. **Which of the following is a mammal?**

a) A snake
b) A bee
c) A sea urchin
d) A whale

2. **Cameroon's national team is known as the Indomitable Lions. What does the word *indomitable* mean?**

a) Impossible to defeat
b) Impossible to dominate
c) Impossible to eat
d) Impossible to catch

3. **Which team has won the Africa Cup of Nations— the competition among the best African teams— the most times?**

a) Egypt
b) Cameroon
c) Ghana
d) Nigeria

4. **Guinea-Bissau's national soccer team is known as the Djurtus. What is a djurtu?**

a) African wild guinea pig
b) African wild dog
c) African wild goldfish
d) African wild tortoise

5. **The Liberian striker George Weah is the only African soccer player to have won the FIFA World Player of the Year Award, which he did in 1995. What new job did he take on in January 2018?**

a) Coach of the Liberian national team
b) Coach of Soccer School
c) Librarian
d) President of Liberia

I did it for you, Mummy!

# POLITICAL SCIENCE

W hich country is famous for bagpipes, berets, and soccer? Not Scotland, not France, but Spain! The country is *mucho* brilliant at soccer, having won the World Cup in 2010 and the Euros three times, most recently in 2008 and 2012. Many top players, like David de Gea, Gerard Piqué, and David Silva, are Spanish.

Spain is made up of many different regions, such as the Basque Country (where they wear berets), Galicia (where they play the bagpipes), and Catalonia (where they dance the *sardana*). In this lesson, we're going to discover how the politics of Spain—that is to say, the way the country is organized into different regions— make its soccer so exciting. Whether in La Liga or on the European stage, the teams are unlike those anywhere else in the world. *¡Bienvenido a España!*

Madrid is the capital of Spain, and the city's biggest soccer team is Real Madrid.

I'm keeping it real!

KING ALFONSO XIII

Originally, the team was called Madrid, but in 1920, the king of Spain allowed the team to incorporate the Spanish word *real* (pronounced ray-AL), which means "royal," into their name. From its early days, the team was associated with the ruling class. It even started to use the crown in its team badge. What a crowning glory!

In the 1950s, Real Madrid won the first five seasons of the European Cup, the competition we now call the Champions League. The team's number one fan, who was prepared to support Real Madrid over other Spanish teams, was the military leader of Spain at the time: General Francisco Franco.

Franco used Real Madrid's success, and the exhilarating way the team played, for his own political goals. His military government was deeply unpopular internationally because it was a **dictatorship**. This style of government is when a person or a small group rules with almost unlimited power and uses force to stop opposition. Franco used Real Madrid's wins to make Spain look as if it were a thriving and exciting country with lots to offer, when actually it was a brutal and dangerous place to be if you opposed his rule.

With such powerful support, Real Madrid became one of the most famous things about Spain. No team has won the European Cup more times than they have, and in 2018, the team was the first to lift the Champions League trophy three seasons in a row. They are also one of the richest clubs in the world. That's real success!

Many people believe that the Spanish government still favors Real Madrid over the country's other teams. Opposition fans complained that during the Franco era, which lasted from 1939 to 1975, referees always favored Real Madrid. In one match against Barcelona in 1966, the referee played eleven minutes of injury time and blew the final whistle as soon as Real Madrid scored the game's only goal. He claimed his watch had broken! Complaints about favorable treatment from referees continue today.

¡Bueno! This is berry, bear-y tasty!

Los blancos

**REAL MADRID**

City population: 3.3 million

Stadium and capacity:
Santiago Bernabéu, 81,044

Most games played:
Raúl González (741)

Fun city fact:
A statue of Madrid's official symbol, a bear standing on its back legs eating strawberries from a tree, stands in the city center.

# RIVAL ACTION

Real Madrid's biggest rival is nearly four hundred miles across the country: Barcelona.

I LoVe cLásico MuSic!

In fact, the competition between the two teams is probably the greatest soccer rivalry in the world—so much so that the match between them has its own name: El Clásico, from the Spanish word meaning "classic," as in "outstanding." The reason why Real Madrid and Barcelona dislike each other so much is a long story . . . so long that it goes back centuries.

Barcelona is the second biggest city in Spain, and the capital of the region of Catalonia. About eight hundred years ago, the region became an independent country—the Principality of Catalonia—with its own laws, language, and customs. But in 1714, after a war, it became part of Spain. At the time, many Catalans did not want to be part of Spain—and more than three hundred years later, some still feel the same way.

The Barcelona soccer team has become a symbol of pride for the region. Barcelona has won more than twenty Spanish league titles and, since 2000, four Champions League trophies. To many fans, every goal Barcelona scores against Real Madrid is a goal for Catalonia against Spain, as if the ancient war between them is still happening on the soccer field.

In recent years, many Catalans have wanted Catalonia to be independent again. The campaign for independence is the reason that if you watch a match at Barcelona's Camp

Nou stadium, you will notice that fans start chanting after seventeen minutes and fourteen seconds, which is to remember the year 1714.

Just as Catalonia has different customs from those in other parts of Spain, Barcelona makes a point of doing things differently from Real Madrid. While Real Madrid often (but not always) buys the biggest soccer stars, known as *galácticos*, from around the world to win trophies, Barcelona focuses on teaching young players a possession-based style of play in its academy. The team encourages coaches to pick these local talents to represent the best of the region. Barcelona's most successful coach, Pep Guardiola, and two of its greatest players, Sergio Busquets and Xavi Hernández, were all born and bred in Catalonia.

Barcelona fans are proud of the differences between them and their great rivals from Madrid—especially when they are winning!

¡Força Barça!

Your beach is a fake, your beach is a faaaaake!

**BARCELONA**

City population: 1.6 million

Stadium and capacity:
Camp Nou, 99,354

Most games played:
Xavi Hernández (869)

Fun city fact:
The city's seven beaches, stretching almost 3 miles/4.5 kilometers, are not natural. They were built for the 1992 Olympic Games.

# BEST OF FRENEMIES

Even though Real Madrid and Barcelona are fierce adversaries, when it comes to the Spain national team, the teams have to put their rivalry aside. It can be difficult to play as a team alongside your archenemies, but the Spanish players have shown it can be done! When Spain won the 2010 World Cup, *nine* of the players who started the final played for either Real Madrid or Barcelona.

This spirit of friendship fell apart, though, after a series of particularly angry Clásico matches in 2011, and defenders Sergio Ramos (Real Madrid) and Gerard Piqué (Barcelona) had a falling out. Luckily, the pair patched things up in time to help Spain win Euro 2012!

Spain has other hotly contested local rivalries all over the country. These derbies are all big games:

| RIVALS | REGION |
|---|---|
| Real Oviedo vs. Sporting Gijón | Asturias |
| Celta Vigo vs. Deportivo La Coruña | Galicia |
| Athletic Bilbao vs. Real Sociedad | Basque Country |
| Sevilla vs. Real Betis | City of Seville |
| Las Palmas vs. Tenerife | Canary Islands |

# WAKE ME UP BEFORE IAGO

Galicia is in the northwest of Spain, close to Portugal. Like other regions, it has its own language, its own customs, and . . . its own weather: this coastal area is famous for being colder and wetter than the rest of Spain. Brrr!

Galicia also has its own fierce soccer rivalry, between teams from the two most populous cities: Celta Vigo from Vigo, and Deportivo La Coruña from nearby A Coruña (*A* means "the" in Galician.) Both used to compete in the Galician regional championship, but General Franco put an end to that competition in 1940.

Celta has never won a major trophy, while Deportivo was nicknamed Súper Dépor when they won their first and only La Liga title in 2000. With little chance of major trophies, these two teams put more emphasis on winning the local derby games—victory counts as a good season for some fans!

One of those fans is Iago Aspas, who grew up in Vigo and started playing for Celta at age eight. He has scored some of the most important goals in the team's history and was top scorer in 2016, 2017, and 2018. He is loved because he has told the fans he will support Celta until the day he dies—and he would not even date a girl from A Coruña. True love!

'Ere Vigo, 'ere Vigo, 'ere Vigo!

CELTA

FOREVER

# BASQUING IN GLORY

The Basque Country is a region in the north of Spain, which is home to Athletic Bilbao, the team that sits third in Spain's all-time trophy table, after Real Madrid and Barcelona. (The Basque Country also extends a little into the southwest border of France.) Athletic is also the only team, apart from the big two, never to have been relegated from La Liga. Its record is particularly amazing because the team picks only players from the Basque Country, which has a collective population of about two million.

The other teams in La Liga choose players from anywhere in the world, which means they can choose from seven billion people. But gutsy Athletic has shown it is a match for the big fish by playing only local talent.

One of the reasons Athletic protects its Basque identity so fiercely is because of the way General Franco tried to stamp out Basque culture in the last century. Franco banned the use of the Basque flag and the use of the Basque language (Euskara) in public. But Franco's plan backfired. Now the Basque language is the region's main language, flags are everywhere, and Athletic Bilbao is one of the strongest symbols of the Basque people. That's why you won't find Athletic ever signing a Brazilian wing-wizard or a tough-tackling Russian defender. It's the Basque way or no way!

How could Athletic Bilbao possibly be so successful with this approach? The team has actually found strength in being so selective:

### 1. Local pride

Athletic players grew up supporting the team and understand the fans because they are fans too.

### 2. Belief in a common purpose

Athletic players know that they don't represent just the team or the city of Bilbao but the whole idea of what it is to be Basque.

### 3. Winning is not the most important thing

Athletic fans want to watch local players on their team — even if they get relegated! Success comes from sticking to the Basque-only policy rather than the number of trophies the team wins.

### 4. Continuity

Athletic mainly promotes players from its youth team, so they already know the area, the team's tactics, and their teammates. Not selling players can be more important than buying new ones!

Ho-ho! I'm happy to go in goal!

## ATHLETIC BILBAO

Bilbao population: 345,122

Stadium and capacity:
San Mamés, 53,289

Most games played:
José Ángel Iribar (614)

Fun city fact:
On Christmas Eve, Basque children celebrate the legend of Olentzero, a stout Basque farmer, who is their version of Santa Claus.

# WE WISH YOU A SMELLY CHRISTMAS

Catalans have a strange Christmas tradition: they put a small figurine depicting a peasant pooping into their Nativity scenes. The tradition dates back to the eighteenth century, but no one is quite sure why it started. Some think the poopers, known as *caganers*, are fertilizing the earth, while others think it symbolizes equality: no matter how famous or successful you might be, you still need to poop. In recent years, Catalan shops have sold celebrity poopers, including members of royalty, American presidents, and, of course, Barcelona players! Poo-ey!

## VANIA ESPAÑA

☆ STAR STUDENT

66 ¡Hola, amigos! 99

## STAR STUDENT Stats

Languages spoken: 7
Preferred Clásico score: 3–3
Regions of Spain visited: 17
Favorite color: Roja
Birthplace: Port of Spain, Trinidad
Supports: La Furia Roja
(The Red Fury, aka Spain)
Fave player: Antonio Valencia
Trick: As nimble as a bullfighter

# POLITICAL SCIENCE QUIZ

1. **What does the Spanish word *real* in the team name Real Madrid mean?**

   a) Rogue
   b) Royal
   c) Real
   d) Rebel

2. **What is the Guggenheim Bilbao, the city's most famous landmark?**

   a) A factory that makes soccer balls
   b) A school where the uniform is the Athletic Bilbao uniform
   c) A museum of modern art
   d) A church where the organ player is the Athletic Bilbao goalkeeper

3. **What is celebrated on September 11 every year in Barcelona?**

   a) Johan Cruyff's birthday
   b) Ham Day
   c) National Day of Catalonia
   d) National Soccer Day

4. **What is the Basque sport of bale-lifting?**

   a) Lifting a bale of hay as many times as possible in a set time
   b) Stealing as many hay bales as you can from a farm before the farmer catches you
   c) Squeezing as many hay bales as possible in an elevator
   d) Lifting Gareth Bale as many times as possible in a set time

5. **What happens at the annual La Tomatina festival in the Spanish town of Buñol?**

   a) More than 20,000 people throw tomatoes at each other in the town square.
   b) All grocery stores give out free tomatoes for a day.
   c) Everyone in Buñol must wear something red for the day.
   d) People named Tom or Tina come from all over the world to dance at a huge outdoor disco.

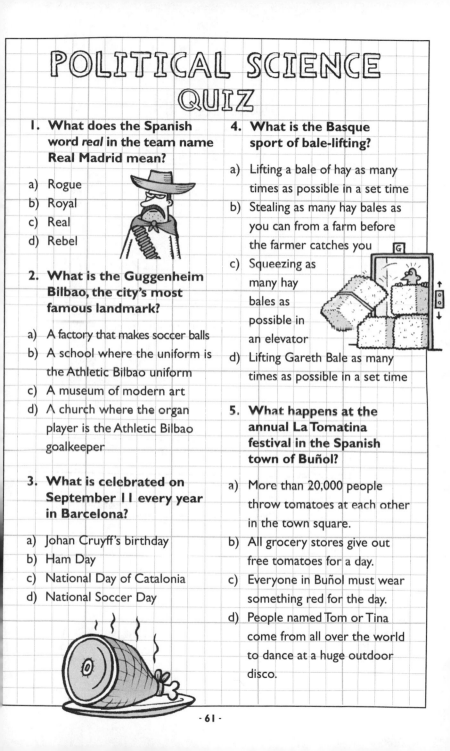

Wakey, wakey! Let's start this lesson with a question: What does everyone need to perform at their best, whether it's Harry Kane getting ready to play in a World Cup game, Alex playing dominoes with Pelé, or Ben running with his dog in the park? No dozing at the back! The answer is: sleep.

*Everyone* needs a good night's sleep, and in this lesson we are going to learn how to get the most out of our z's. Professional soccer players have to play games at all hours: at lunchtime, in the afternoon, and even late at night. They need to be getting enough sleep to be alert no matter what time it is.

We're going to find out what tricks they use to get the best night's sleep before a big game. We'll also meet the man who tells Real Madrid's players what pajamas to wear. And we'll learn about an animal that sleeps for only two hours every day.

Rise and shine!

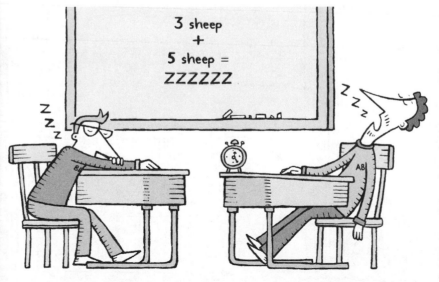

# SLEEPY HEADS

When we go to sleep, we feel our mind slowly drifting off
. . . and off . . . and off . . . Meanwhile, our body is getting to
work, because when you sleep, a lot of things are happening.

☾ The heart slows, blood pressure lowers, the body's
temperature drops, and the blood supply to the
muscles increases. This helps restore our energy levels
for when we wake.

☾ Chemicals are released to repair injured cells. This
helps the body protect itself against illness and
recover from injury.

☾ The part of the brain that stores memories reviews
things that happened that day.

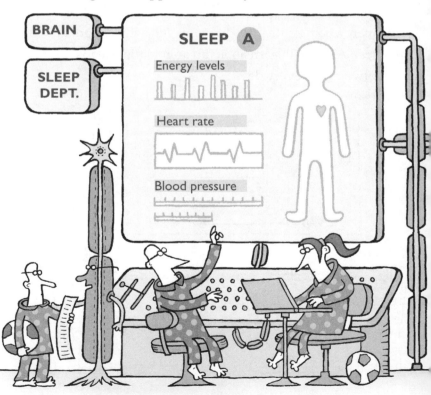

Sleep is our daily recovery and rejuvenation routine. Recently, scientists have discovered just how important sleep is, not only to our health but also to our happiness. They say that the right amount of sleep can help us live longer and be happier, more driven and creative, and even more honest. Tell that to your parents when they try to wake you up!

Sleep can make a massive difference to athletes too. Players who sleep soundly have better reaction times and decision-making skills and also recover more quickly from injury than those who toss and turn. Before we meet the man who teaches soccer players how to sleep, let's learn about what happens when we are counting sheep. . . . *Baa*-ck to bed!

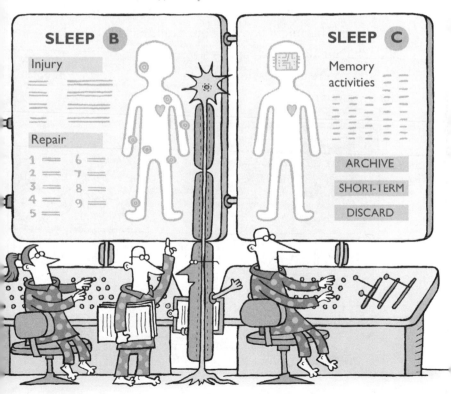

# FIVE-A-NIGHT

When you're asleep, your body goes through a cycle of four different stages. Each stage serves a specific purpose, and each complete cycle lasts around ninety minutes — the same time as a soccer game!

You go through many **sleep cycles** in a night. Doctors say that four-year-olds need about twelve hours of sleep a night, eight- to twelve-year-olds need about ten hours, and adults need about eight hours.

But it is not just about the number of hours; it is also about the quality of the sleep. **Deep sleep** is the most restorative sleep for your body, and the longer that period is, the better you will feel the next day. Babies spend a lot of time in deep sleep. But the older you become, the longer your **light sleep** cycle lasts. This might be why your grandparents complain about having had a bad night's sleep.

So if you're a professional soccer player, how do you get the most out of your z's?

# SLEEP DIARY

## Stage 1: TRANSITIONAL PHASE

About 5 minutes

The mind drops off. The eyes might roll.
The muscles might jerk as you enter a light sleep.

FUNCTION: To prepare the body for sleep.

## Stage 2: LIGHT SLEEP

About 45 minutes

The muscles relax, the mind rests, and the heart rate slows down. You can be easily woken from this stage.

FUNCTION: To repair damaged cells.

## Stage 3: DEEP SLEEP

About 20 minutes

This is the most refreshing part of sleep. Breathing slows. The body is still. Sometimes your limbs will move, so this is when sleepwalking, talking in your sleep, or bed-wetting can occur.

FUNCTION: This is the key stage for your body and mind to recover. The brain gets a reboot so it can learn afresh the next day. If you are a child, this is when your body grows.

## Stage 4: REM (Rapid Eye Movement) SLEEP

About 20 minutes

The brain is active and revitalized. The body is still, apart from your eyelids, which flutter. The heart rate and blood pressure increase. You dream. The length of this stage increases with each cycle, so longer dreams occur toward the end of sleep.

FUNCTION: To store memories as the brain processes our emotional experiences.

## ASLEEP ON THE JOB

Nick Littlehales was working for a mattress company when he wrote to former Manchester United coach Sir Alex Ferguson, offering to help players recover from games with sleep advice. Ferguson was keen to know more. Littlehales suggested that defender Gary Pallister, who was suffering from back problems, change his mattress. His advice also helped Ryan Giggs play for United even after he had turned forty.

That's how Littlehales started his new job as a sleep coach for the world's biggest soccer teams, including Chelsea, Real Madrid, and the England national team.

Our body regulates its own feelings of sleepiness and wakefulness according to natural light. When it is dark outside, we are more likely to want to sleep. When it's light, we want to be active. Littlehales visits each player's bedroom to make sure the player has a good set of curtains and doesn't have too many distractions. One player he visited had four different flat-screen TVs on his bedroom wall, while another had a huge lit-up aquarium. Lights-out!

# TEACHING RONALDO TO SLEEP

When Littlehales was at Real Madrid, he knew that Cristiano Ronaldo was looking to improve all aspects of his performance, including his recovery and sleep. Littlehales gave tips to the players and coaches at Real Madrid and is proud that Ronaldo has adopted the principles of his advice. This is what Littlehales told European soccer's most successful team:

☾ Switch off all devices—such as laptops, smartphones, and tablets—more than an hour before you go to sleep. The blue light from these devices triggers brain waves, which make it harder to go to sleep.

☾ Move from a warm, light area to a cooler, darker one. This re-creates the everyday process of sunrise and sunset as your brain slowly relaxes from hyper-awake mode.

☾ Avoid fatty or sugary foods in the evening, as they take longer to digest. A balanced diet, which includes carbohydrates such as pasta and protein such as chicken and nuts, will improve sleep quality.

☾ Sleep in the fetal position, which is like a baby curled up in their mother's stomach. This protects your vital organs. Lie on your nondominant side. If you are right-handed, lie on your left side: this position leaves your strong side free.

# EARLY BIRDS AND NIGHT OWLS

We're all different—and this is also true when it comes to sleep. Alex likes to get up at a time so early that most of us are still asleep. He's an early bird. Ben prefers to go to bed later and wake up later in the morning. He's a night owl. What are you?

Your preference for certain sleeping patterns is based on an internal clock inside your body. This is known as your body clock, or **circadian rhythm**. Studies have shown that athletes reach their peak performance depending on their circadian rhythm. This information can be important for coaches, as it will help them get the best out of their team.

| SLEEPING PATTERN | BEST PERFORMANCE |
|---|---|
| Early Bird | 6–7 hours after waking up |
| Night Owl | 11 hours after waking up |

# SIESTA FIESTA

We didn't always save sleep for one long session at the end of the day. Historians believe humans used to sleep for a bit, then get up in the middle of the night to do tasks before going back to sleep again. Some experts believe that this is still the best way for the body to regularly recover. In certain cultures, particularly in hot countries like Spain or Greece, a midday nap is normal. This is known as a **siesta**. Swansea City has even encouraged its players to take daytime naps by installing sleep pods at the training center.

# CLEAN ROOM, CLEAN MIND

Some people count sheep; others read until they drop their book. But England's current record goal scorer, Wayne Rooney, used to put on the vacuum cleaner before he went to sleep! The repetitive and monotonous sound it made, known as **white noise**, drowned out other sounds that might keep him awake. When that didn't work, he would use his girlfriend's hair dryer—sometimes until it broke!

## SLEEPOVER

The majority of athletes find it difficult to fall asleep before a big event. One team, Southampton, used to take custom-made mattresses to hotels for away games, so players would be used to the beds despite the unfamiliar environment. Another team, Bournemouth, gives its players a sleep pack containing amber-lensed glasses, an eye mask, and a small flashlight. The glasses, to be worn two hours before going to sleep, block out the blue light from TVs and devices. The eye mask keeps out the light once the players are asleep. The flashlight gives enough light so if players wake up in the middle of the night, they can go to the bathroom without turning on the main lights.

# COUNTING SHEEP

Animals also need different amounts of sleep. Look at how long certain species sleep in a twenty-four-hour cycle:

Did you see that goal?

No, sorry, I must have nodded off!

| ANIMAL | AVERAGE LENGTH OF SLEEP (PER 24 HRS.) |
|---|---|
| Giraffe | 2 hours |
| Horse | 3 hours |
| Elephant | 4 hours |
| Python | 18 hours |
| Aldabra tortoise | 18 hours |
| Brown bat | 20 hours |

WILLOW PILLOW

STAR STUDENT

zzz

66 Sweet hat-trick dreams! 99

STAR STUDENT Stats

Sheep counted per night: 221
Pairs of pajamas: 14
Room temperature: 68°F/20°C
Flat-screen TVs in bedroom: 0
Birthplace: Sleepy Hollow, NY
Supports: Santiago Morning (Chile)
Fave player: Ryan Moon
Trick: Sleepwalks through the defense

# HEALTH QUIZ

1. **The dream stage of sleep is called REM. What does REM stand for?**

   a) Really Extraordinary Memories

   b) Rest, Exhale, Motionless

   c) Rapid Eye Movement

   d) Ready for Exciting Missions

2. **How does Manchester City keep its recovery rooms dark so players can rest properly?**

   a) All the light bulbs are removed.

   b) There are blackout curtains over the windows.

   c) The rooms are underground.

   d) It makes the players wear blindfolds.

3. **What was French midfielder Julien Faubert accused of doing when playing for Real Madrid against Villarreal in 2009?**

   a) Missing the game by falling asleep in his car on the way to the stadium

   b) Falling asleep in the locker room at halftime

   c) Falling asleep on the substitutes' bench

   d) Falling asleep on the field as soon as the final whistle blew

4. **How long did Ghana midfielder Michael Essien, a Premier League title winner with Chelsea, say he needed to sleep every night?**

   a) 4 hours

   b) 8 hours

   c) 10 hours

   d) 14 hours

5. **What causes snoring?**

   a) Your nose farting

   b) Lying in an uncomfortable position

   c) Your throat or nasal airways vibrating as you breathe

   d) Reading a Soccer School book before bed

**SOCCER SCHOOL**

## VISIT TO FOREST GREEN ROVERS SOCCER CLUB

Dear Parent/Guardian,

Your child is going on a field trip. The topics that will be covered include the following:

Burping cows

Farting bugs

Flushing toilets

**Mode of transport:** electric bus

**Please bring:** notepad made from recycled paper, biodegradable garbage bag

**Don't bring:** plastic packaging, pets, soccer balls
A lunch of fungus will be provided. Water will be available all day, served in recycled plastic bottles.

Kind regards,
Alex and Ben

I give permission for ........................................ to take part in the field trip and promise that they will limit the singing of soccer songs on the bus trip, refrain from playing soccer using cow pies, and will make a list of green goals at the end of the day.

Parent/Guardian signature:........................................

We're traveling today to Nailsworth, a small town in the countryside of Gloucestershire, England. It's the home of Forest Green Rovers, a team that in 2017 was promoted to the English Football League for the first time in its history.

Forest Green is very different from any other team—not just in England, but anywhere in the world. It likes to do things their own way. In fact, if you look out the bus window, you'll see that the team is so concerned about being different that the name of the road that leads to the stadium is called Another Way!

Forest Green wants to do things differently by looking after the planet as much as possible.

# SOCCER TO THE RESCUE

Forest Green wants to save the world! But before we get off the bus and begin our visit to the team, let's look at two reasons the world needs saving in the first place.

## PROBLEM 1: CLIMATE CHANGE

The world is heating up, which is causing many problems. The ice at the North and South Poles is melting, which means that polar bears may soon lose their home. We can't bear it! And, because the water from the melting ice is going into the world's oceans, the height of the sea, or **sea level**, is rising. If the sea level continues to rise, many villages, towns, and cities all over the world could flood and eventually go underwater. Glug!

The major cause of **climate change** is the burning of fuels such as oil and coal. (These substances are known as **fossil fuels** because they are made over millions of years from dead plants and animals being crushed and heated underground.) When fossil fuels are burned, they create a gas—carbon dioxide—that ends up trapping heat in Earth's atmosphere, making the planet hotter.

## PROBLEM 2: PLASTIC POLLUTION

Plastic is fantastic! It is long-lasting, cheap, and useful for so many things. But these reasons also make plastic really bad for the environment. For example, huge amounts are thrown away every day, and since it is long-lasting and does not rot, it ends up in rivers, on beaches, and in the oceans, where it is a danger to sharks, fish, whales, and other marine animals. The plastic problem is drastic!

## CHANGE THE WORLD

We could reduce the problem of climate change if we stopped burning oil and coal. And we could greatly reduce the problem of plastic pollution if we stopped using things made from plastic.

Sounds easy! But it is impractical and unrealistic to think we can instantly give up oil, coal, and plastics. We'd also have to give up traveling by plane, ship, and most cars, since they use gasoline. And we use plastics every day in hundreds of ways, from our toothbrush to our water bottle. Our way of life relies on substances that are damaging the world.

But we need to look after our planet better than we have been. We are going to have to change our behavior by reducing our dependence on fossil fuels and throwing away less stuff that may be harmful to animals.

Forest Green Rovers is leading the way in doing both of these things—and more. Let's start our first worksheet and find out how.

# WORKSHEET 1: ENERGY

The electricity that we use when we switch on the lights comes from many different energy sources. In the United States, almost two-thirds of the electricity comes from burning fossil fuels; in Canada, the figure is about 20 percent. Fossil fuels are **nonrenewable**, which means that they will run out and take millions of years to be replaced. But electricity can also be made from **renewable** sources, which will not run out and can be used again and again. One shining example is the sun!

A **solar panel** is a shiny panel that absorbs sunlight and turns it into electricity. The New Lawn, the Forest Green stadium, has 170 solar panels on its roof, which provide the team with free electricity.

The advantages of solar power are that sunlight is free and the panels create no fumes or waste gases when they are used. The disadvantage is that it needs to be sunny! Sunny countries have lots of solar panels. The largest single "farm" of solar panels is in India and covers an area about the size of 6,500 soccer fields.

Other renewable sources of energy include the following:

☐ Wind       ☐ Waves       ☐ Heat from below the ground

# WORKSHEET 2: PESTICIDES

In order to grow as much food as possible, farmers often use chemicals on their crops. **Fertilizers** help the crops grow, and **pesticides** kill weeds and bugs that might eat the crops. The same is true of a soccer field. To get perfect luscious green grass, most grounds crews also use fertilizers and pesticides.

But many fertilizers and pesticides contain chemicals that are harmful to humans and animals. Pesticides can kill insects such as bees, which are important to the environment. And, when the chemicals enter the soil, they don't just stay there. They get washed into rivers and may ultimately end up in the ocean, where they can harm fish. Traces can even be found in drinking water.

At Forest Green, the grounds crew doesn't use pesticides, and It uses only fertilizers that are not harmful to humans and animals. These three options are all on the menu:

☐ Tea for bugs, who then fart out gas that strengthens the roots

☐ Vinegar to kill off weeds          ☐ Sugar and seaweed to feed the grass

# WORKSHEET 3: SAVING WATER

A guiding principle of Forest Green is that we should never waste resources. Waste not, want not! That's why the team collects its own rainwater. Some is saved from the stadium roof and some from sloping drains below the field, which flow into a water tank managed by groundskeeper Adam Witchell. The water tank can hold up to 19,000 gallons/73,500 liters, which is enough water to fill more than six hundred bathtubs.

Adam aims to collect enough rainwater for free so that he can water the field using the team's own reserves without ever switching on a faucet. Last season he almost managed it. The only time he turned on a faucet was during a summer heat wave.

At Soccer School, we agree with Forest Green's message of never wasting water. Most of us use a huge amount of water every day without realizing it. One way to cut down on water is to always take a shower rather than a bath. Look how much water you save:

☐ Bath: 𝛿𝛿𝛿𝛿𝛿𝛿𝛿𝛿𝛿𝛿𝛿𝛿𝛿𝛿𝛿𝛿𝛿𝛿𝛿𝛿𝛿𝛿𝛿    30 gallons/ 115 liters

☐ Shower: 𝛿𝛿𝛿𝛿𝛿𝛿𝛿𝛿𝛿    13 gallons/ 50 liters

☐ Toilet flush: 𝛿    1½ gallons/ 6 liters

# WORKSHEET 4: EATING GREEN

Fancy a hamburger at halftime? Sorry, you're out of luck!
At Forest Green, meat and fish are banned. Instead, hungry fans
are offered a Q-Pie, which is made from Quorn, a well-known meat
substitute that is made from a fungus.

Meat is banned because of the effect that the meat industry has
on the planet. Farming animals uses a lot more land, feed, and water
than farming the same amount of vegetables and grains. The high cost
to the planet of eating meat has made some people decide to eat no
meat products at all. People who don't eat meat are **vegetarians**,
and people who don't eat meat or any other animal by-products,
such as eggs and milk, are called **vegans**. Here are three international
foods that many vegans love:

☐ Tofu:

Semisolid soybean milk,
originally from China

☐ Quinoa:

Tiny plant seeds used
as an alternative to rice,
originally from the
Andes Mountains

☐ Freekeh:

A nutty grain also used
as an alternative to rice,
originally from the
Eastern Mediterranean
and North Africa

Cows are especially bad for the environment because of their
burps! Cows belch a gas called **methane**, which, like carbon dioxide,
makes the world get hotter. There are about 1.4 billion cows in the
world, and the combined mega-burp of 1.4 billion cows is big,
as well as stinky!

PARP!

BURP!

# WORKSHEET 5: POLLUTION

Gasoline-powered cars release carbon dioxide and dangerous chemicals that can cause breathing problems in humans. This is known as **air pollution**.

In the last few years, car companies have been designing cars that run on electricity, which creates no exhaust fumes at all. Some drivers already using electric cars are ... the players of Forest Green Rovers, after a company gave each of them an electric car for six months.

Electric cars are still more expensive than gas cars, so fewer people drive them, but it is likely that this will change in the next ten years or so. In the near future, it's predicted that most cars will be fume-free.

Forest Green Rovers isn't gas-free just on the road, but on the field too. They use a self-driving lawn mower that uses GPS to figure out where it's going. It doesn't run on gas, as many stadium lawn mowers do, but instead on solar-powered electricity. If it bumps into an object, it backs up and mows somewhere else. It takes three days to mow the entire field, and it will text the grounds team if it gets into trouble. We hope it uses an e-mow-ji!

# SOCCER SCHOOL GREEN GOALS

To finish off our trip to Forest Green, we spoke to Dale Vince, the owner of Forest Green Rovers. "We care deeply about the environment and want to show that soccer can also care for the world around us," he said.

The team is helping to protect the planet by recycling as much as it can, not putting harmful chemicals into the ground, limiting the amount of carbon dioxide pumped into the air, and using renewable sources, such as sunlight and rainwater. Often people use the word *green* to describe these types of environmentally friendly activities. FIFA has called Forest Green the greenest team in the world!

Dale told us that the team can become even greener, which is why he wants to build a new stadium made almost entirely out of wood. Wood is a renewable material, since trees can be replanted, unlike concrete and steel. Go, Dale—we be-leaf in you!

This trip has taught us that we can all become greener. Here's a checklist of green goals that can help the planet. What else can you add to the list?

- **Reuse plastic bottles**
- **Recycle all paper**
- **Walk or bike instead of using a car**
- **Turn the TV off after *Sports Center***

# WHAT A LOAD OF GARBAGE

Cristiano Ronaldo scored both goals when Real Madrid beat Sporting Gijón in the Spanish league in November 2016—but some people thought he looked like total trash! The reason? Real Madrid was wearing shirts made from plastic garbage that had been found on the coast around the Maldives Islands in the Indian Ocean. They had the message "For the oceans" on the neck of the shirt. The team was highlighting an important cause: when you throw plastic away, it can end up in the ocean, where it can kill marine animals. It can cause problems for humans too: if we eat fish that has swallowed plastic, we could become sick as a result. A solution: make sure you recycle your plastic bags and bottles; don't throw them in the garbage!

**LIV GREENE**

⭐ STAR STUDENT

66 Let's recycle possession! 99

STAR STUDENT Stats

Daily water use: 2½ gallons/ 10 liters
Weekly intake of tofu: 4½ pounds/2 kg
Solar panels on roof: 5
Plastic toys: 0
Birthplace: Greenland, NH
Supports: Forest Green Rovers, England
Fave Player: Son Heung-Min
Trick: Brings sunshine to the ☆ dressing room

# FIELD TRIP QUIZ

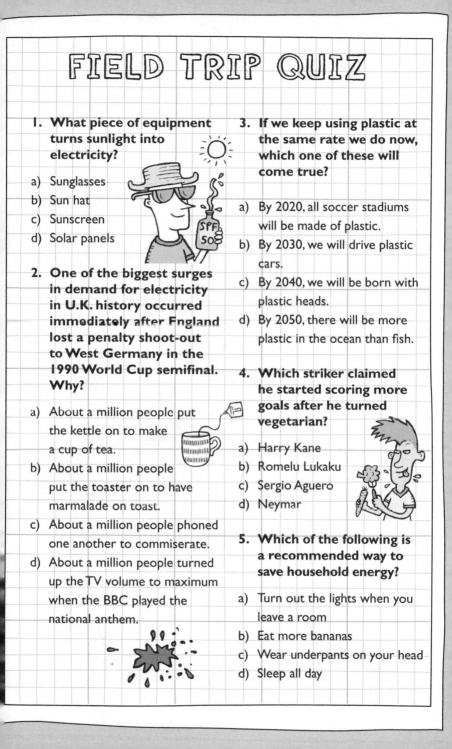

1.  **What piece of equipment turns sunlight into electricity?**

    a) Sunglasses
    b) Sun hat
    c) Sunscreen
    d) Solar panels

2.  **One of the biggest surges in demand for electricity in U.K. history occurred immediately after England lost a penalty shoot-out to West Germany in the 1990 World Cup semifinal. Why?**

    a) About a million people put the kettle on to make a cup of tea.
    b) About a million people put the toaster on to have marmalade on toast.
    c) About a million people phoned one another to commiserate.
    d) About a million people turned up the TV volume to maximum when the BBC played the national anthem.

3.  **If we keep using plastic at the same rate we do now, which one of these will come true?**

    a) By 2020, all soccer stadiums will be made of plastic.
    b) By 2030, we will drive plastic cars.
    c) By 2040, we will be born with plastic heads.
    d) By 2050, there will be more plastic in the ocean than fish.

4.  **Which striker claimed he started scoring more goals after he turned vegetarian?**

    a) Harry Kane
    b) Romelu Lukaku
    c) Sergio Aguero
    d) Neymar

5.  **Which of the following is a recommended way to save household energy?**

    a) Turn out the lights when you leave a room
    b) Eat more bananas
    c) Wear underpants on your head
    d) Sleep all day

# HISTORY

For this lesson, we're going back in time: way back to Sheffield, England, in the 1850s, when two smart people had an idea that changed the world. Can you guess what it is? It has brought joy and sometimes sadness to millions of people all around the world. Nope, it's not Soccer School. But without these two pals, Soccer School might not exist.

Let's step into the time machine!

# WHERE IT BALL BEGAN

One sunny day in the summer of 1857, two friends went for a walk in the countryside just outside the city of Sheffield in the north of England. William Prest, a twenty-five-year-old wine merchant, and Nathaniel Creswick, a twenty-six-year-old lawyer, were both athletic and loved sports.

On this particular walk, they chatted about two of the most popular sports of that time: fencing and cricket. They also talked about a new sport, football (also known as soccer), which was being played at schools, such as Eton, and universities, such as Cambridge. Each school had its own version of the rules, and before every game, the captains would agree on the rules for that particular match. But imagine a game in which the rules changed slightly every time you play—confusing!

The friends decided that football would be a good sport for the people of Sheffield—if there were some organized rules that every team could follow. So they wrote to all the schools to find out their rules. "What a lot of different rules we received," Creswick later wrote. There wasn't even a defined length of time for matches. "We generally played until it was dark," one school reported.

The friends took the best suggestions and started to write down a version of the rules they were both happy with. A few months later, on October 24, 1857, they founded Sheffield Football Club, the first soccer club in the world. The club's purpose was to get people together to play soccer during the winter months, when no one was playing cricket.

In 1859, Prest and Creswick finalized their rule book, which they handed out to all members of their new club. Here are some of the rules:

## The Rules of Football

### 1859

- The kickoff from the middle must be a placekick.

- Pushing with the hands is allowed, but no hacking or tripping up is fair, under any circumstances whatsoever.

- The ball may be pushed or hit with the hand, but holding the ball except in the case of a free kick is altogether disallowed.

- Each player must provide himself with a red and dark-blue flannel cap. One color to be worn by each side during play.

# GOLDEN RULES

The Sheffield Football Club rule book from 1859 is the foundation of the game as we know it today. Only once there were written rules that everyone agreed on could soccer grow from schools and universities to become a national—and then a global—sport.

Some of the rules have changed since 1859, such as the ones about pushing the ball with the hands or wearing flannel caps, but even so, creation of the rule book was a landmark moment in soccer history. It set the future course for the game, most notably because, even though the ball could be pushed and hit by the hands, *holding* the ball was forbidden. Until this point, catching the ball with the hands was a key part of the rules followed by Cambridge University. Soccer historian Andy Dixon told us that without the Sheffield rules, the game we love today might look more similar to rugby, where holding the ball is allowed. Handball, ref!

*Sheffield rules? But I'm from Cambridge!*

# LIGHTS, HEADERS, ACTION!

William Prest and Nathaniel Creswick were pioneers. The word *pioneer* was originally used for soldiers who marched ahead of their regiment to prepare the way, but it is now used for people who are the first to explore regions or introduce new ideas. And did those pals like to innovate! In addition to the rule book, Sheffield FC introduced other important elements of the game.

## Headers

In 1866, Sheffield played London City at an away game at Battersea Park. The London team could not stop laughing when the visitors used their heads to pass the ball to each other in the air. It was not forbidden in the rules, but it was the first time any team had used headers. This was also the first game to be played for an agreed-upon ninety minutes.

## Floodlights

Two Sheffield players captained the teams in the first game played under floodlights, in 1878 at Bramall Lane.

## Derby Matches

Sheffield played Hallam on December 26, 1860, and the idea of local rivalries got started. These two clubs still play soccer's oldest derby match today.

## Throw-ins, Corner Kicks, Halftime Change of Ends

Thanks to Sheffield FC, the city became the national hub for soccer, home to about one-third of the first one hundred teams to play the game. Other Sheffield innovations include throw-ins, corner kicks, and changing ends at halftime.

# SHEFFIELD OF DREAMS

In order to understand why the first soccer team was founded in Sheffield, rather than anywhere else in Britain or the world, we need to consider how the world of work had been changing for the previous hundred years.

In the 1750s, most working people made things using their hands. But by the 1850s, a new type of workplace had emerged: the factory. One of the most important things made in factories was steel, the metal that was used for railroads, ships, and machines. Sheffield became the world center of steel production. It was located in an area rich in iron ore, which is the mineral that steel is made from. In 1850, 85 percent of the steel made in the U.K. was from Sheffield, and it was exported all around the world. Sheffield—nicknamed the Steel City—became rich. Its wealth and industry turned Sheffield into a center of innovation, just the sort of place where people wanted to try a new sport.

## LIGHT-BULB MOMENTS

In the mid-nineteenth century, many new ideas—besides organized soccer—changed the world. Here are some:

| YEAR | INVENTION | INVENTOR |
|------|-----------|----------|
| 1846 | Sewing machine | Elias Howe (USA) |
| 1876 | Telephone | Alexander Graham Bell (USA) |
| 1879 | Light bulb | Thomas Edison (USA) |

Life without soccer is now just as unthinkable as life without the sewing machine, telephone, and light bulb.

## HOORAY FOR THE WEEKEND

Another mid-nineteenth-century invention was the weekend. Before the existence of factories, people in the U.K. generally worked six days a week, with only Sunday off. Factory workers in places such as Sheffield, however, were allowed Saturday afternoons off too. Soccer was able to grow because all of a sudden people had leisure time when they could play and watch a game.

# LOVE OF THE GAME

Sheffield FC was an **amateur** club, meaning that it did not pay its players. The club wanted the team to play only for the love of the game. In the 1880s, however, some clubs in the city became professional, meaning that their players earned money.

Sheffield FC's decision to stay amateur meant that most of their best players went to play for other teams. For example, when Sheffield United decided to start paying their players in 1889, more than half of the men who turned up for the first trial were from Sheffield FC! It was not long before Sheffield FC was eclipsed by the professional teams in the city, such as Sheffield United and Sheffield Wednesday.

But while United and Wednesday might make more money and have more fans, they can never say they were the first team in the world.

## THAT'S YOUR LOT

Sheffield FC raised more than £880,000 (about $1.3 million) in 2011 by selling the original rule book, which contained the printed *Rules, Regulations, & Laws of the Sheffield Foot-Ball Club* (as it was written then) from 1859. The buyer was anonymous. The club might have been hoping for a bit more money: the original document explaining the rules of basketball fetched £2.6 million ($4 million) at an auction in New York in 2010!

# HAPPY BIRTHDAY!

Sheffield FC celebrated its 160th birthday in 2017. "Our founders created the team for the love of the game and we have worked hard to protect that," said club chairman Richard Tims. "In essence, no matter what team you support, this club is your club's great-grandfather."

Today, the club has a men's team that plays in English soccer's eighth division, the Northern Premier League. It also fields another twenty teams across all age levels, including five women's teams. These days, the women overshadow the men when it comes to success on the field. Sheffield's women's first team was formed in 2003, starting in the bottom league. Sheffield FC Ladies kept winning and ended up with six promotions in the space of just eight seasons. In 2015, Sheffield FC Ladies beat Portsmouth 1–0 in a playoff match to reach the top division, the Women's Super League, for the first time in their history.

# OLDIES BUT GOLDIES

Sheffield FC is the oldest club in the world. Here are some of the oldest clubs in other places:

| CLUB | DATE FORMED | WHERE |
|---|---|---|
| Wrexham | 1864 | Wales |
| Queen's Park | 1867 | Scotland |
| St. Gallen | 1879 | Switzerland |
| Koninklijke | 1879 | Netherlands |
| Cliftonville | 1879 | Northern Ireland |
| Royal Antwerp | 1880 | Belgium |
| Hong Kong | 1886 | Hong Kong |
| North Shore United | 1886 | New Zealand |
| Germania | 1888 | Germany |
| Recreativo de Huelva | 1889 | Spain |
| Genoa | 1893 | Italy |
| Le Havre | 1894 | France |
| Rio Grande | 1900 | Brazil |

NEIL McSTEEL

STAR ☆STUDENT

66 Sharpen up! 99

☆ STAR ☆☆ STUDENT Stats

Flannel caps: 22
New ideas per day: 5
Days worked per week: 5.5
Spoons in collection: 300
Birthplace: Yellowknife, Canada
Supports: Metalurh Donetsk (Ukraine)
Fave player: Luke Steele
Trick: Moves like quicksilver

# HISTORY QUIZ

1. **What product was Sheffield famous for making in the 1800s?**

a) Rubber
b) Brass
c) Steel
d) Gold

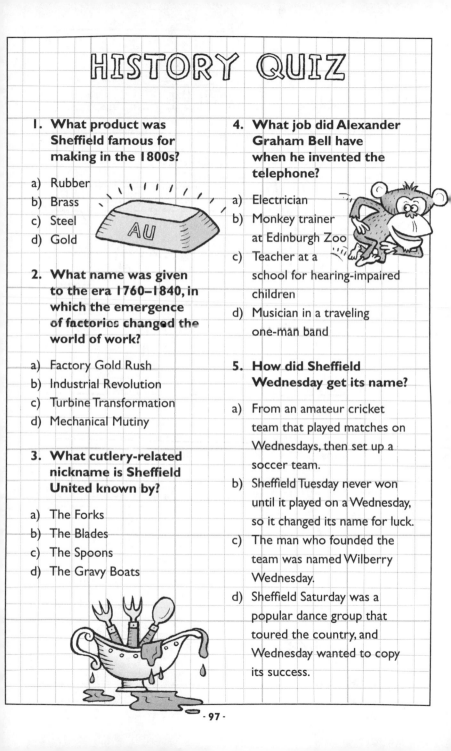

2. **What name was given to the era 1760–1840, in which the emergence of factories changed the world of work?**

a) Factory Gold Rush
b) Industrial Revolution
c) Turbine Transformation
d) Mechanical Mutiny

3. **What cutlery-related nickname is Sheffield United known by?**

a) The Forks
b) The Blades
c) The Spoons
d) The Gravy Boats

4. **What job did Alexander Graham Bell have when he invented the telephone?**

a) Electrician
b) Monkey trainer at Edinburgh Zoo
c) Teacher at a school for hearing-impaired children
d) Musician in a traveling one-man band

5. **How did Sheffield Wednesday get its name?**

a) From an amateur cricket team that played matches on Wednesdays, then set up a soccer team.
b) Sheffield Tuesday never won until it played on a Wednesday, so it changed its name for luck.
c) The man who founded the team was named Wilberry Wednesday.
d) Sheffield Saturday was a popular dance group that toured the country, and Wednesday wanted to copy its success.

MATH

That's not fair!" How many times have you shouted that while watching a game? Soccer, like all sports, relies on fairness.

We want the rules to be applied fairly, meaning that no team is favored over another. We want the players to respect the rules and show compassion and respect to the other players and fans. This is called **fair play**.

But there is another sort of fairness, which we will be talking about in this lesson. What is the fairest way of deciding between two teams who have shown themselves to be equal? For example, how can league standings be decided when two teams have the same number of points?

Methods used to decide between teams include goal difference, away goals, head-to-head results, and, amazingly, even the flipping of a coin. Flipping heck! Heads or tails, anyone?

| P | W | D | L | GF | GA | P |
|---|---|---|---|----|----|---|
| 11 | 8 | 1 | 2 | 35 | 6 | 2 |
| 11 | 7 | 3 | 1 | 38 | 12 | 2 |
| 12 | 7 | 1 | 4 | 29 | 12 | 2 |
| 10 | 6 | 3 | 1 | 17 | 9 | 2 |
| 11 | 5 | 2 | 4 | 19 | 18 | 1 |
| | | | 3 | 21 | 18 | 1 |
| | | | 5 | 18 | 16 | 1 |

# FREAKY FRACTIONS

Alex loves looking at league tables. One reason he likes them is because the numbers are always whole numbers, such as 1, 22, and 43. Whole numbers are neat and simple.

What you never see in a league table is a **fraction**, such as 1.818 or 1.794. You need to think harder with fractions.

But Alex loves a bit of fraction action! They are on (decimal) point!

Until about forty years ago, every soccer fan was also fanatical about fractions. League tables were full of them because back then there was a column for **goal average**, which is:

> the number of goals scored
> divided by the number of goals let in

So, if your team scored 60 goals by the end of the season and let in, or **conceded**, 33, they would have a goal average of

$$60 \div 33 = 1.818$$

And if they scored 61 but conceded 34, the team would have a goal average of

$$61 \div 34 = 1.794$$

Sounds confusing! Just think of goal average as being the number of goals you score for every goal you concede. So, a goal average of 1.794 means that, on average, you score 1.794 times for every goal you let in. Awe-sum!

$$61 \div 34$$

# TIED UP

For almost a hundred years, goal average was the **tiebreaker** used in soccer leagues, meaning that if two teams were equal on points, the one with the higher goal average would be placed above the one with the lower goal average.

For example, Huddersfield Town and Cardiff City both finished the 1923–1924 season at the top of the English First Division, each with 57 points. (The First Division was the forerunner of the Premier League.)

But Huddersfield had a 1.818 goal average, compared to 1.794 for Cardiff. So Huddersfield was crowned champion by just 0.024. Eek!

Back then it paid to be good at math if you were a soccer fan. In 1923, there were no pocket calculators, smartphones, or computers, so most people would have calculated goal average on paper, using long division. Frac-attack!

# DIFFERENT SYSTEM

The tiebreaker now used in the Premier League to separate two teams with equal on points is **goal difference**, which is:

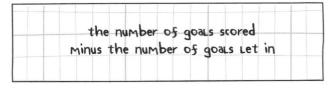

the number of goals scored
minus the number of goals let in

Goal difference tells you how many more goals you have scored than you have conceded. The system was introduced in the 1970s because it encourages teams to play more exciting soccer. We can do some addition to see why.

Imagine Alex and Ben each have a team. At the end of the season, the teams have played twenty games each and have the same number of points but the following goal records:

|  | GAMES PLAYED | GOALS FOR | GOALS AGAINST | GOAL AVERAGE | GOAL DIFFERENCE |
|---|---|---|---|---|---|
| TEAM ALEX | 20 | 80 | 40 | 2 | 40 |
| TEAM BEN | 20 | 25 | 10 | 2.5 | 15 |

If we use goal average, Team Ben is better than Team Alex. But if we use goal difference, Team Alex is better than Team Ben. Who should come first in the table? Tense!

Now, which team has played the most exciting soccer? Surely it is Team Alex, which has scored more than twice the number of goals as Team Ben. In fact, the system was changed to favor high-scoring teams, like Team Alex, over low-scoring teams, like Team Ben.

Is goal difference a fairer way to separate two teams than goal average? It depends on your point of view.

Here at Soccer School, we think goal difference is fairer to the fans because it encourages more goals. Defensive-minded coaches, on the other hand, may think that goal average is fairer.

Whichever one is fairer, when it comes to the calculations, goal difference is certainly easier!

## BREAKOUT

Not every country uses goal difference. In Spain, ties are broken by looking at the results of games between the two teams, and in Argentina, if the top teams have equal points, they will face a playoff. At Soccer School, we've come up with some great ideas for tiebreakers.

Dance-off

2. Alex's incredibly complicated formula

$$\sum_{n=1}^{M=\infty} \sqrt[n]{\left[\frac{da}{dx} \times \frac{x^2}{\pi}\right]}$$

3. Tidiest bed

4. Best-looking goalie

# THE GREAT WORLD CUP LOTTERY

Luigi Franco Gemma was a fourteen-year-old Italian boy who took part in one of the strangest events in the history of the World Cup. In March 1954 at Rome's Olimpico stadium, he was blindfolded and asked to place his hand in a trophy cup and select one of the two pieces of paper inside.

One of the pieces of paper was marked *Spain* and the other *Turkey*. His choice would determine which of these two countries qualified for the 1954 World Cup in Switzerland.

The room was packed with the Spanish and Turkish teams and officials from FIFA. Luigi put his hand in the cup, grabbed one of the pieces of paper, and it was . . . Turkey!

The Turkish delegation was overjoyed because they were headed to the World Cup. The Spanish delegation was devastated, since they were not.

The practice of making decisions by having someone reach into a hat or a bowl and choosing one of several items randomly is called **drawing lots**. It is an ancient custom often used to settle disputes. The lots are the items in the selection—and this is where the word *lottery* comes from.

Drawing lots is seen to be the fairest way to make a choice when all other options have been exhausted because if the choice is made randomly, each lot has the same chance of being chosen.

Spain and Turkey had both finished at the top of their World Cup qualifying group, which led to the teams playing a decider in Italy. But the game finished 2–2 after extra time, and the rules said that in the event of a draw, the winner would be decided by drawing lots.

In snatching the qualification, Turkey had lots to celebrate! They treated Luigi like a hero and even invited him to accompany the squad to the World Cup, as they thought he would bring them good luck.

For Spain, however, the result was not a lot of fun. Even though drawing lots is part of the rules, it never feels fair to have your destiny decided by something beyond your control.

# FISHY BUSINESS

Luigi Franco Gemma's fateful choice in Rome was the first and last time that a team has failed to get to the World Cup based on drawing lots. However, the World Cup itself has witnessed the drawing of lots twice since then, in 1970 and 1990.

In 1990, the tiebreakers for teams finishing tied for points in the groups stage were the following:

## 1990 WORLD CUP TIEBREAKERS

1) The team with the best goal difference
2) The team that has scored most goals
3) The winner of the match between those two teams
4) The drawing of lots

The tiebreakers are done in order, so only once goal difference has been taken into account will goals scored be considered, and so on.

In 1990, Ireland and the Netherlands both topped their respective group with the same points, the same goal difference, and the same total goals scored, and they had drawn the match against each other 1–1. Lots had to be drawn in order to establish which team was placed above the other.

Two yellow balls (one for Ireland and one for the Netherlands) were put in a goldfish bowl, and two red balls (with two numbers) were put in another bowl. A ball was chosen from each. The result: Ireland placed above the Netherlands.

Using lots to choose between teams may be the fairest way if all other channels have been explored, but it is never as fair as basing the decision on something that happened on the field. The World Cup now has an extra tiebreaker: the team's disciplinary record. In the 2018 World Cup, this method was used to separate Japan and Senegal.

The Champions League has twelve tiebreak rules for the group stages, including club coefficient, a number based on results over the previous five years. Everything is done to avoid the goldfish bowls—and the anger of fans.

# THE LONG AND SHORT OF IT

Soccer is not the only arena where the final option is the drawing of lots. In some political elections, if the two candidates with the most votes have an equal number of votes, the winner is decided by lots. This happened in the U.K. in a local election for Northumberland County Council in 2017. To decide the winner, the election official put a long straw and a short straw in his hand, with the same length of straw visible. The candidates had to each choose a straw, with the candidate who chose the long straw being declared the winner. That's why we often say we drew the short straw when we have bad luck.

# TOSS-UP

Perhaps the most common form of leaving a decision up to chance is flipping a coin, since the idea behind both is that the chances of any outcome are equal. When you flip a coin, the likelihood of it landing heads is almost the same as the likelihood of it landing tails.

Coins are used at the beginning of every soccer game. One of the team captains chooses heads or tails, the referee tosses the coin so it lands on their hand or on the ground, and the winner of the toss decides which goal their team will attack in the first half.

But did you know that coin tosses also used to happen at the end of soccer games? Before the introduction of penalty shoot-outs, coin tosses were used to decide the winners of knockout matches in competitions like the European Cup, which was the top European competition before the Champions League.

For example, in 1965, Liverpool drew 2–2 with Cologne in the quarterfinals, but Liverpool qualified because they won the coin toss. In 1969, in the second round of the same competition, Celtic beat Benfica on a coin toss after their scores were 3–3 on aggregate.

The heartache for fans when these big games were decided by the flip of a coin was one of the main reasons for the introduction of the penalty shoot-out. By the end of the 1970s, penalty shoot-outs had been adopted by the European Cup, the European Championship, and the World Cup. Out with the penny; in with the penalty!

# ABBA-DABA-DOO

Using a penalty shoot-out to decide the winner requires more skill than guessing heads or tails. Yet how fair are penalty shoot-outs?

The traditional system for penalty shoot-outs is that the teams take penalties one after the other, so if the teams are A and B, the order for the first five rounds is AB AB AB AB AB. Once these five are taken, the team that has scored the most wins. If the scores are even, the teams take penalties in the same order until one scores and the other doesn't.

Ben is a penalty expert. He knows that penalties are not very fair because the team shooting first wins 60 percent of the time on average, and the team shooting second wins only 40 percent of the time. In other words, it's an advantage to shoot first. This is because there is more pressure on the team kicking second, especially toward the end of the shoot-out, when players know that missing the penalty will lead to defeat.

Mathematicians have devised a new system to make shoot-outs fairer. The order of the teams is switched each round: the first five kicks of each team are AB BA AB BA AB. By switching the order every two kicks, the advantage of shooting first is more balanced. The "ABBA" system may become standard in shoot-outs in the future.

# COOL COINS

In ancient Rome, coins were flipped as a way of settling disputes. If the coin landed showing the face of leader Julius Caesar, it was thought that he agreed with the decision.

Around 1900, the statistician Karl Pearson flipped a coin 24,000 times in order to see what the split was between heads and tails. The result: 12,012 heads and 11,988 tails. This works out to be 50.05 percent vs. 49.95 percent.

Mathematicians in the United States investigating coin tosses built a coin-flipping machine and estimated that a coin will land on its edge once every six thousand throws.

STAR ☆ STUDENT

LOTTIE LUCK

66 I'll take a chance! 99

☆ ☆ ☆ STAR STUDENT Stats

Pet goldfish: 2
Packets of straws: 3
Coins: 40
Heads or tails: Heads. No, tails!
Birthplace: Las Vegas, Nevada
Supports: Fortuna Düsseldorf (Germany)
Fave player: Chancel Mbemba
Trick: Always unpredictable

# MATH QUIZ

1. **How do you calculate goal difference?**

a) Goals scored + goals let in
b) Goals scored − goals let in
c) Goals scored x goals let in
d) Goals scored ÷ goals let in

2. **What happened when referee Svein Oddvar Moen tossed a coin at the beginning of a Norwegian league game in 2015?**

a) The coin hit the head of one of the captains.
b) He flipped the coin into his own mouth.
c) He used a joke coin with two heads.
d) He is a professional magician so made the coin disappear.

3. **Which of the following is NOT used as a tiebreaker in the Champions League?**

a) Away goals
b) Fair play
c) Fart average
d) Club coefficient

4. **If two coins are flipped, what is the percentage chance that both land on heads?**

a) 0 percent
b) 25 percent
c) 50 percent
d) 100 percent

5. **What did Danish assistant coach Søren Randa-Boldt say when Denmark knocked Russia out of the 2013 Women's Euros on the drawing of lots?**

a) "The Viking god Thor hammered it for us tonight!"
b) "Lady Luck smiled on the Lucky Ladies!"
c) "This was the easiest match of our lives!"
d) "I feel for Russia; it's horrible for them. But we're happy and we're ready."

# GEOGRAPHY

Brrrr! Wrap up warm, as we are going to one of the coldest and least populated countries in the world. Iceland is a small island almost halfway between the United Kingdom and the North Pole. It's famous all over the world for its extraordinary landscape of geographical wonders — including active volcanoes, huge waterfalls, and beaches of black sand — and its millions of puffins!

ICELAND

FASTER! FASTER 1-2 1-2

But we're already puffin'!

Recently, the country has also become known for its extraordinary national soccer team, which achieved a remarkable feat. In 2018, Iceland became the smallest country in terms of population ever to play in a World Cup. In this lesson, we're going to see how these modern-day Vikings have overcome the challenges of freezing temperatures, dark nights, and a small population to become a team to watch. Huuh! Huuh! Huuh!

# THE LAND OF ICE, FIRE . . .

Iceland is a freezing wilderness of rock, ice, and fire. There are two reasons for this: a plume and two plates. The Iceland plume is a hot spot of boiling rock lying almost 2,000 miles/3,200 kilometers beneath the earth's surface, directly below Iceland. **Geologists**, the scientists who study rocks, believe Iceland was formed millions of years ago when that hot spot erupted and molten rocks, or **lava**, rose to the ocean surface, before cooling and turning into the island.

The plates are **tectonic plates**, which are huge pieces of the earth's crust. Iceland is positioned on the border of two major tectonic plates that are moving apart at a speed of 1 inch/2.5 centimeters per year. It doesn't sound like much, but that's more than 15 miles/24 kilometers every million years. As the plates move apart, they cause openings for molten rock to burst through. Mountains created by the lava that spurts out are called **volcanoes**. Iceland has 130 volcanoes, and one of them will erupt approximately once every four years.

When Iceland's volcanoes erupt, the rest of the world knows about it. One eruption in 2010 released a huge cloud of ash that made it impossible for planes to fly across Europe. Thousands of flights were canceled, and millions of passengers were stranded. One canceled flight was booked by Barcelona for its Champions League semifinal tie against Inter Milan. Because the team couldn't fly to Italy, they traveled the 600 miles / 965 kilometers by bus instead. The players were tired when they arrived in Italy, and they lost the game 3–1. What a pa-LAVA!

Iceland's volcanic activity also means there are bubbling pools of hot water or vents of steam, known as **geysers**, all over the country. Iceland's capital, Reykjavik, translates as "Smoky Bay," a name that dates from the time Viking settlers arrived more than a thousand years ago and found hot springs that produced steam. Some of these hot springs are the temperature of a warm bath, so despite the cold, you can have an outdoor soak all year round. Don't forget your towel!

But Iceland is not named after its hot parts. Ten percent of the country is covered by **glaciers**, which are vast sheets of slow-moving ice. Glaciers are formed over many years when snow doesn't melt but turns to ice. The ice sheets are constantly moving under their own weight. Freezy does it!

Hey, geyser, is this the way to the hot springs?

# . . . AND FAKE GRASS

Being so far north means the days in Iceland vary dramatically in length. In the summer, it gets dark for only a few hours each night. But in the winter, it is light for just a few hours a day. In the middle of December in Reykjavik, for example, the sun rises after 11:00 a.m. and sets around 3:00 p.m. The dark, along with the snow and ice, makes it difficult to play soccer outdoors in Iceland all year round.

To solve this problem, the Icelandic Football (Soccer) Association came up with a plan to build as many indoor artificial fields as possible. There are now almost 150 indoor arenas, which are heated and well lit so the weather and darkness can't stop play. "There is now an artificial field close to almost every school in Iceland," said the former national team coach Heimir Hallgrímsson. There are also more than 600 UEFA-qualified coaches, who work on improving children's technique from the age of three upward. That translates to one coach for every 550 Icelanders, which is an amazing ratio. Good facilities + good coaches = good skills!

# SMALL YET STRONG

Perhaps the greatest challenge to Iceland having a good national team is the number of Icelanders.

The United States has a population of about 327 million, Brazil has about 210 million, England has 53 million, and Scotland has 5 million. Yet Iceland's population is only 340,000 —about the size of a medium-size city, such as St. Louis.

In fact, the entire population of Iceland is equivalent to just over four full Michigan Stadiums!

How on earth do you get a team good enough to qualify for the World Cup from such a small pool of talent? Our friend Kristján Jónsson, a soccer writer based in Reykjavik, says it comes down to several reasons:

 Icelanders are descended from the Vikings and come from generations of fishermen and farmers. Growing up doing physical work in harsh weather conditions builds a tough attitude.

 The Iceland players have all played alongside one another since they were young, so they know one another very well. That team spirit is a big advantage.

 Icelanders understand the value of teamwork. In a small community, no one likes a show-off! "You can't act like you're better than anyone else," says Kristján.

 The small size of the island means community is strong. The team celebrates with the fans because they are fans too.

# THE ICEMEN COMETH. . . .
## MEET THE TEAM

Here is the inside scoop on the team that brought Iceland to the 2018 World Cup: it's a story of kicks, cameras, teeth, and tenacity.

## THE FREE-KICK EXPERT

Gylfi Sigurdsson is Iceland's most famous player. He has played in the English Premier League for Tottenham Hotspur, Swansea, and Everton, and he is known as one of the best free-kick takers in the world. He has won Icelandic Player of the Year for six years in a row. Sigurdsson's older brother Olafur helped improve his technique from the age of five, and his dad once rented a warehouse in the winter so the boys always had somewhere to play. Practice really does make perfect!

## THE FILM-MAKER

Playing soccer in Iceland is only a part-time job, which means that some players need another job to earn money when they are not on the field. Goalkeeper Hannes Thór Halldórsson makes films: he made his first when he was twelve years old. Since then, he has directed Iceland's music video (about an elf) for the 2012 Eurovision Song Contest (Iceland finished twentieth!) and a video for Iceland's national airline, which starred his teammates—and himself! He also worked on a horror film that he described as a "supernatural ghost thriller that takes place in an isolated part of Iceland." Spooky!

Hey! I'm down here!

# THE DENTIST

Heimir Hallgrímsson alternated his role as Iceland national team coach at the 2018 World Cup with his other job as a professional dentist in his hometown of Heimaey. Seeing his patients allowed him to take his mind off soccer for a while. And calming his patients' nerves before they went into his dentist chair helped him practice telling the players not to be nervous before games. "As a dentist, you have to treat a patient who might be scared," he said. "Probably it's the same with players. You speak to them in different ways too." Now that he's left his coaching job, he can go back to being a dentist. Open wide and say "Aaah!"

# THE FANS

Heimir Hallgrímsson is unique in world soccer for another reason. Many teams call their fans the twelfth player, but the relationship between Iceland fans and their team is closer than most. When he was assistant coach, Hallgrímsson used to meet fans before games to explain the lineup and tactics. "It's something that makes us different, and I really believe it has strengthened the connection between the supporters and the team," Hallgrímsson explained. He did the same even when he was head coach. "I see going to the pub with the fans and then meeting the team at the stadium as my prematch routine now." Imagine Pep Guardiola or José Mourinho doing the same!

# THUNDERING SUCCESS

This connection remains strong after games, when Iceland players approach the fans and perform a ritual "Thunderclap." The players raise their arms out wide and, starting slowly, do a single clap over their heads. As their hands connect, they shout "Huuh!" The fans copy them. Gradually, the speed and volume of the clapping and chanting increases, rising to a thunderous crescendo. Give those fans a big hand!

Some people thought the chant went back to ancient times when the inhabitants of Iceland were Vikings, but the truth is not quite so historical. Twenty-two fans of Icelandic club Stjarnan went to watch their team play Scottish team Motherwell in a 2014 European game. Motherwell fans performed a version of the Thunderclap that the Stjarnan fans took home with them. The Iceland team's fans liked it so much that they adopted it with their own players. The volume of the clap and bond it helps create between fans and players is the envy of teams worldwide.

# ICE QUEENS

Icelanders believe that women and men should be given the same opportunities in life. At Soccer School, we also believe in gender equality! Iceland recently came first in a survey ranking gender equality across the world. So it's no surprise that Iceland's women's team is also incredibly successful. It reached the European championship quarterfinals in 1994 and 2013, and in 2017, it became the first team in nineteen years to beat Germany in a World Cup qualifying match.

## THE NAME GAME

Icelanders don't have family names. Instead, men usually use the name of their father appended with -*son*, meaning "son," and women use the name of their father, appended with -*dóttir*, meaning "daughter." For example, Gylfi Sigurdsson is so called because he is the son of Sigurd. The all-time leading scorer for the Iceland women's team, Margrét Lára Vidarsdóttir, is so called because she is the daughter of Vidar. Some people use their mother's name, like former Icelandic forward Heidar Helguson, son of Helga. Alex and Ben's Icelandic names would be Alex Davidson (father's name) and Ben Andreason (mother's name). What's yours?

# ELF AND SAFETY

The majority of people in Iceland believe that the country is also home to an invisible tribe of elves called *Huldufólk*, meaning "the hidden people." Construction work on a road in Reykjavik was stopped when protesters warned it would disrupt elves living in a rock formation that believers call the Elf Chapel. "You can't live in this landscape and not believe in a force greater than you," said Adalheidur Gudmundsdottir, a professor of folklore at the University of Iceland.

STAR STUDENT

RICK E. VICK

"Huuuuuhhh!"

STAR STUDENT Stats

Elves under bed: 5
Minimum sunlight hours: 5
Woolly sweaters: 43
Annual intake of fish: 1 ton
Birthplace: Chile
Supports: Viking (Norway)
Fave player: Tom Heaton
Trick: Form can run hot and cold

# GEOGRAPHY QUIZ

1. **What does the name of Iceland's capital city, Reykjavik, mean in Old Norse?**

   a) Land of Puffins
   b) Home to Volcanoes
   c) Smoky Bay
   d) Bring extra socks

2. **Which of the following letters are not in the Icelandic alphabet?**

   a) O, M, G
   b) C, Q, W
   c) G, O, L
   d) X, Y, Z

3. **Which of the following can you find in Iceland:**

   a) Expressways
   b) McDonald's restaurants
   c) Mosquitoes
   d) Ice cream

4. **What was special about Vigdís Finnbogadóttir, Iceland's president from 1980 to 1996?**

   a) Her previous job was coach of the Iceland women's soccer team.
   b) She was the world's first elected female president.
   c) She played goalkeeper for Iceland while serving as president.
   d) She was a famous pop star.

5. **Iceland forward Eidur Gudjohnsen won two Premier League titles with Chelsea and the Champions League with Barcelona. Why was his Iceland debut a family occasion?**

   a) His uncle was Iceland's coach at the time.
   b) He came on as a substitute and replaced his dad.
   c) His brother was playing for the opposition.
   d) His grandfather was goalkeeper.

This lesson will be more exciting than watching paint dry.

Actually, this lesson is going to *be* about watching paint dry!

Paint is a colorful subject. It is a fascinating and important material, and the world depends on it. Look around you and you will see paint: on walls, doors, ceilings and window frames, cars, signs, roads, buildings, planes, trains, ships, and more.

When you are watching a game of soccer, you are also watching paint: the bright-white lines that mark the boundary of the field, the boxes, and the center circle.

In this lesson, we will find out about what goes into paint, why it is like cake (yes, you read that right), and how it is applied on the grass of a field.

Let's paint the town red! No, we mean paint the grass white!

## THE WHITE STUFF

In soccer's distant past, fields were often marked using . . . weed killer!

Weed killer left ugly yellow lines of dead grass. Horrible! Grounds crews also used paint made from a white powder called **lime**, but lime sometimes burned players' skin.

These nasty substances aren't used anymore. Fields are now marked using brilliant-white paint that allows the grass to live and players to avoid rashes. A-grazing!

There have been many other advances in paint technology since the bad old grass-murdering, skin-burning days, but before we get there, put on your chef hat and apron, because we are going into the kitchen.

## GREAT CHEMISTRY

The study of how substances interact with one another is called **chemistry**. But did you know that all baking is chemistry? When we bake a cake, the different ingredients we put in the mixing bowl interact with one another to eventually become cake.

At Soccer School, we love eating cake. (Especially Ben!) We also love cake because it explains to us how paint works. We don't mean that you can eat paint or stick candles in it. Warning! Please do not eat paint!

But let's look at how the chemistry of paint is just like the chemistry of cake. On your mark, get set, bake!

# MAGIC SPONGE CAKE

To make a cake, you must assemble various ingredients, mix them, and then bake the mix in the oven. When it comes out, the mix has turned into a solid cake. It tastes and smells delicious. Here's how Ben likes to make cake:

| BEN'S CAKE OF CHAMPIONS | |
| --- | --- |
| INGREDIENTS | METHOD |
| Eggs | 1. Create mixture. |
| Flour | (Assemble and mix ingredients.) |
| Butter | ? Apply mixture to desired |
| Sugar | location. (Pour it into a cake pan.) |
| Nuts | 3. Mixture undergoes a chemical |
| Raisins | change. (Bake it in the oven.) |
| Dates | |
| Carrots | |

As the mixture turns into cake, each of the ingredients plays a role. The eggs, flour, butter, and sugar make the sponge. The nuts, raisins, and dates give the cake flavor. The carrot fills out the cake and gives it texture.

The most important part of the cake is the sponge, since the sponge binds everything together. If there were no sponge, there would be no cake. Once the mixture is put in the oven, the heat causes chemical changes to take place, and the gooey mess solidifies into the finished cake. Yum!

# CAUGHT IN A BIND

Now let's think about paint. It's mixed in a factory and comes in a can. You dip in a brush, brush the paint onto a surface, and then wait for it to dry. The process is actually very similar to making a cake (although the main ingredients aren't food but chemicals we call **binder**, **pigment**, and **filler**):

**PAINT**

| INGREDIENTS | METHOD |
|---|---|
| Binder | 1. Create mixture. (Assemble and mix ingredients.) |
| Pigment | |
| Filler | |
| | 2. Apply mixture to desired location. (Brush or spray paint it onto a surface.) |
| | 3. Mixture undergoes a chemical change. (Leave it to dry.) |

Each of the three chemical ingredients does something different. The binder, which is transparent, binds all the other ingredients together. (It's like the sponge in the cake.)

The pigment provides the color (just as the nuts and raisins add flavor).

The filler fills out the paint and may change the texture (just like the carrot).

Paint starts off as a liquid and undergoes a chemical change, ending up as a solid layer of color. The process of paint drying is so similar to the process of cake baking that chemists consider drying a type of baking that happens at room temperature. Those curious chemists!

# FAN FAVORITES

# ALL IN THE MIX

By tweaking a cake's ingredients, you can change its characteristics. For example, you can make it fluffier, denser, or more moist. Likewise, by tweaking the three ingredients of paint, you can change its characteristics. Paint is used for many things, and each of them has different requirements. Look at these examples:

### For field markings:

1) Must be visible from a long distance
2) Must not kill the grass
3) Must be waterproof
4) Must look good for a week or so but doesn't have to last longer than that

### For stadium walls:

1) Must last for years, since you don't want to repaint the walls every week
2) Must be waterproof, because the walls will be rained on
3) Must be durable, as the walls will get scuffed by fans walking next to them

### For your bedroom:

1) Must last for years
2) Must be available in lots of colors
3) Does not need to be waterproof, since it doesn't rain indoors
4) Must be able to be cleaned with a cloth, as you might spill or splatter something on the wall

# THIS LITTLE PIGMENT

When you watch a soccer game, you may be watching players who have traveled to the stadium from different countries. And you may also be watching paint that has put in some miles.

This is because the white pigment used in white paint is the chemical titanium dioxide, which comes from **ilmenite**, a substance found in sand and rock. And the biggest sources of ilmenite in the world are in Australia, South Africa, Canada, and Mozambique. Rock on!

# PITCH PERFECT

When a movie star gets ready for a photo shoot, they will get their hair and makeup done. The same thing happens when a professional soccer field gets ready for a game. But for hair, think grass, and for makeup, think paint. The goal in both cases is to look as attractive as possible.

At about 8:00 a.m. on a game day, the grounds team will give the field a trim by mowing it. This takes a couple of hours. Then it's time to prepare it for painting. The first step is to "string out" the field, meaning that pegs are placed at the ends of the lines that will be painted, and the string is pulled taut along the lines. The string acts as a reference so that when the lines are painted, they are straight.

Small and amateur clubs tend to use painting machines that look like a golf cart with three wheels. Paint pours onto the middle wheel, which marks the line on the grass as the wheel rolls along. Because the wheel rolls the grass stems flat, only one side of the stem is painted, so the line has to be repainted in the other direction too. Then the line is wheelie good!

Top teams now use machines with spray paint: the paint is blown out of a tiny nozzle as a fine mist. This method does not flatten the stems, and the paint gets on both sides in one spray, meaning that you need to paint the line only once. The mist method also delivers—and requires—only a very thin layer of paint. In fact, it is possible to use only 4 cups / 1 liter of paint to mark up an entire field, although teams usually use around 2½ gallons / 10 liters so that the white is as bright as possible.

Once the field is painted (the entire process, including stringing out, takes about an hour and a half) it is left to dry. Spray paint dries in about twenty minutes, but wheeled-out paint needs more time. Once the paint is dry, the string is removed so it doesn't trip the players when they come on the field. No one wants to be tackled by a piece of string! Once the paint is dry, the field is watered and left for a couple of hours before the players warm up on it.

## RAIN, RAIN, GO AWAY

The biggest enemy of field paint is rain! If it's raining buckets, you get problems. Paint applied on wet grass will mix with the water and become thinner, so the white will be less bright. Watery paint won't stick to the stems, so it will run off into the soil. Rain also means that the paint won't dry as quickly, and, in some cases, it will rub off onto the players. One groundskeeper we spoke to said that one time, the lines didn't dry in time and when the goalkeeper dived, he ended up with a white shirt and white hair. "He aged forty years in ninety minutes!" the groundskeeper said. The grounds crew is always checking the weather forecast and hoping game days are dry. They may even paint the lines the night before if it means avoiding a shower.

# GOLD STANDARD

Soccer teams are always blaming bad results on referees. But top Chinese team Guangzhou R&F once blamed the paint. Guangzhou plays in blue, and their stadium used to be blue. But after a run of bad results, the team decided to repaint the entire stadium gold. And it seemed to work. When it was blue, the team had only one home win in four months, but when the stadium was gold, Guangzhou won its next five games in a row. Goooaaald!

**MATT WHITE**

☆ STAR STUDENT

66 Dab it on! 99

☆☆☆ STAR STUDENT | Stats

Dries in: 1 hour
Number of coats: 3
Smudges: 132
Favorite celebration: The Dab
Birthplace: Paignton, England
Supports: Glossop North End (England)
Fave player: John Paintsil
Trick: Runs in a very straight line

# CHEMISTRY QUIZ

1. **What is the name of the substance that gives paint color?**

a) Piglet
b) Pigtail
c) Pigeon
d) Pigment

2. **What is the total length of the white lines that must be painted around the Wembley field, which is 115 yards/105 meters by 75 yards/69 meters?**

a) 190 yards/174 meters
b) 266 yards/243 meters
c) 381 yards/348 meters
d) 459 yards/420 meters

3. **Which of these is a common filler for paint?**

a) Socks
b) Chalk
c) Cheese
d) Carrots

4. **What paint nightmare happened during a game in 2016 between MLS rivals Montreal Impact and Toronto?**

a) The match was delayed by thirty minutes while the grounds team repainted the penalty box lines.
b) It started to rain hard, washing away the paint marks and leaving the linespeople unable to tell if a ball was in or out.
c) The paint hadn't dried in time, and by the end of the game, footprints could be seen all over the field.
d) The grounds crew ran out of white paint halfway through painting, so the penalty boxes were painted in red.

5. **Titanium dioxide, a chemical used in white paint, is made up of titanium and which other substance?**

a) Hydrogen
b) Oxygen
c) Oxtail
d) Oxlade-Chamberlain

FASHION

People are always changing their clothes.

That's to say, people are always changing their minds about clothes. Alex used to love wearing flip-flops, but now he always wears sneakers. Ben used to love his striped pajamas, but now he prefers the ones with polka dots. Why do we change our minds about what we wear? Surely, as long as our clothes keep us warm and are comfortable, it shouldn't matter how they look.

But we've all had a moment where we've wanted a piece of clothing that is new and different from what's in our closet. In this lesson, we're going to learn about fashion and soccer uniforms. We'll admire some classic shirt designs and laugh at some hideous ones.

Looking good!

# AFTER A FASHION

We change our opinions about the clothes we wear for many reasons, such as when we:

- See something we like online, in a magazine, on TV, or in a store
- Get bored with what we are wearing and want something new
- See a friend wearing something cool

We say an item of clothing is **in fashion** if it is very popular, and **out of fashion** (like Alex's old flip-flops) if it is unpopular. Clothes can go in and out of fashion quickly. One day, everyone in class might be wearing red socks, and then, a few weeks later, no one would be caught dead in red socks. These fashion moments, when everyone copies the same look, are called **trends**.

No single person decides what will be in fashion. Rather, it depends on many factors, such as what's on TV, what's in stores, how much money it costs, what celebrities (including soccer players) are wearing, what new fabrics scientists have invented, or even what the weather is like.

# TRENDSETTERS

Clothes companies try to create trends in order to sell more clothes, but it doesn't always work. Fashion and trends can be hard to predict!

One reason things go in and out of fashion is human psychology. We like to feel that we fit in with our friends, and wearing the same clothes as them is an obvious way to show the world that we have things in common. This is why people love to wear band T-shirts or the jersey of their favorite team. Fashion can make you feel as though you belong in a group.

But we also like to stand out to show people that we are different and special. It's a delicate balance. No one wants to look as if they've just copied their friend or a celebrity. Often when an item of clothing becomes too popular, people stop wearing it, since wearing something everyone else is wearing shows a lack of individuality.

Fashion is like a big wheel, with things always coming into fashion, going out of fashion, and then coming back into fashion. One day, Alex may even wear his flip-flops again!

# FASHION FORWARDS

Soccer players are not afraid to try new fashions. Here are some we applaud for trying to stand out:

### Dani Alves

This Brazilian loves brightness in his fashion choices, from gold sneakers with teddy bears on the tongue to shiny jackets with artistic prints. Our favorite outfit of Dani's came before a Champions League tie in 2015: a red tuxedo, black bow tie, black shorts, and rhinestone-encrusted suede loafers with the image of *Batman*'s the Joker on them.

No wonder he moved to Paris, the home of fashion, in 2017!

### Mario Balotelli

When asked who his most stylish teammate was, this Italian replied, "Me." He specializes in eccentric headgear, from the hoodie with its own Mohawk to the "glove hat," a brown-and-yellow woolen beanie with five fingers sticking up along the top of his head.

### David Beckham

The former England captain wore a sarong over a pair of black pants during the 1998 World Cup. He did not regret it, even if people at the time joked: "How can anything that seems so right be sarong?"

**Megan Rapinoe**

This American midfielder set up her own clothing brand with twin sister, Rachael, to help people stand up for what they believe in. Rapinoe supports women's rights, LGBTQ+ rights, and racial justice, and her clothes have messages that sum up her approach to life: be authentic and help others do the same. One of her T-shirts says: BE YOUR BEST YOU!

# THE KIT CATWALK

Soccer uniforms (or "kits") are a great way of seeing how trends keep changing and often come full circle. Sometimes shirts with collars are in fashion, sometimes V-necks are all the rage, and at other times crew necks are the style. Sometimes shorts only just cover players' butts, and at other times they reach down to their knees.

Clubs like updating team uniforms every year for many reasons. A new, exciting design makes players look and feel special, promising a glorious future. (Don't you always feel good when you put on brand-new clothes?) A new uniform also means that the club can sell more replica shirts, since fans always want to have the latest item. But uniform designs also respond to wider changes in society. Here we'll see that the introduction of floodlights, the invention of new fabrics, and the rise of the European Cup (now what we call the Champions League) are all things that have influenced what soccer players wear.

# A SHORT HISTORY OF SOCCER UNIFORMS

## 1900s TO 1930s: KNEESY DOES IT

At the beginning of the last century, tight-fitting shirts with vertical stripes were the big trend. They had long sleeves and were usually made from heavyweight cotton. The most popular style was a crew neck (a rounded neckline) with laces. A rule requiring players to cover their knees was abolished, so for the first time in soccer history, knees were on display—and shorts reached to just above them. Knee-t! The dyes used for clothes at that time were not colorfast, so soccer shirts would look more and more washed out as the season went on.

Women's soccer became popular during World War I. Sometimes women wore the same uniform as the men, but sometimes they wore very different ones that included full- or calf-length skirts. They wore caps in the team colors to keep their hair up.

## 1930s TO 1950s: BUTTONS UP

The first World Cup was played in 1930, by which time no one wanted a crew neck anymore. The most common shirt style in the U.K. had a collar and buttons down the front. Below the waist, shorts became baggy and there was a trend of horizontal stripes on socks. Hoop hoop hooray!

## 1950s: LIGHTWEIGHT

A few years after the end of
World War II, which lasted
from 1939 to 1945, English
and Scottish clubs started to
play against European clubs
in tournaments, such as the
European Cup. Many of these

European teams were better than the British teams, and
they wore much more lightweight uniforms. As a result,
the Brits copied their look. Out went the heavy collars and
baggy shorts, and in came slick V-necks, short sleeves, and
shorter shorts. Heavy woolen socks became a thing of the
past and were replaced by lightweight nylon ones.

## 1960s: BRIGHT WHITE

The 1960s were a period of
great cultural change and
artistic creativity. New pop
bands like the Beatles wore
clothes that were neat and
unfussy, and this trend was
reflected in soccer. Shirts now
had basic crew necks and
long sleeves. The introduction
of floodlights led to several
clubs adopting all-white
uniforms—white shirts, shorts,
and socks—which stood out
particularly well.

## 1970s: FLARE FOR FASHION

If you look at photos of bands from the 1970s, you will see big hairstyles, bold colors, glitter, and flared pants. Soccer fashion embraced this sense of excess. In England, shirts featured long, droopy collars and decorative stripes down the side of the arms. And the hair! England's best player, Kevin Keegan, became as famous for his poodle haircut as for his skills.

## 1980s: MATERIAL MANIA

New materials and manufacturing techniques radically changed the look and feel of soccer shirts. Artificial fabrics like polyester were much lighter than the traditional cotton and didn't get heavy with sweat. It was also possible to produce very intricate designs, like pinstripes and shadow stripes. The V-neck style was favored. Players were allowed to choose whether to wear long or short sleeves, except at Arsenal, where it was the captain's decision.

## 1990s: OFF-PITCH STYLE

At the end of the twentieth century, it became fashionable for fans to buy replica shirts and wear them to games. Then fans started to wear the replica shirts all the time, at home and when out with friends. As a result, teams started to design soccer shirts made to look good with jeans. This period was

the most creative time for shirt designers. They introduced lots of new colors, such as powder blue and silver gray, and designed many inventive patterns, such as splotches, wavy stripes, and even tiger stripes.

The first Women's World Cup was held in 1991, and the women's game became more popular throughout the decade. Women's uniforms in general have the same style as the men's.

## 2000 TO NOW: SKINTIGHT

In the 2000s, the outlandish designs of the previous decade settled down and the styles became simpler again. Style trends are now seen as less important than making sure that the latest advances in fabric technology make uniforms as light and water resistant as possible. Shorts became really long and baggy—at one point down to the knees, a length not

seen for a hundred years—but are now rising again. Another recent innovation by some shirt manufacturers is super-skinny designs that fit like shrink-wrap.

# SOCCER SCHOOL'S WARDROBE OF WACKINESS

Welcome to our collection of curious and interesting shirts from around the world. Most teams prefer plain colors or stripes. But not all . . .

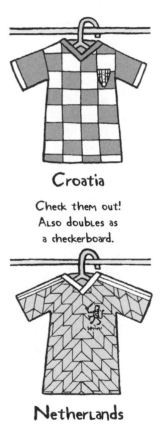

### Croatia

Check them out!
Also doubles as
a checkerboard.

### Hull City

In 1992, the Tigers
roared with these stripes.

### Netherlands

In 1988, the Dutch
were unparalleled in their
use of parallelograms.

### Peru

The Peruvians love
to sashay with a sash.

### Arsenal

In 1991, Arsenal's yellow away uniform was nicknamed the "bruised banana."

### USA

Painted by hand? No, USA's 1994 World Cup uniform had wobbly stripes.

### Mexico

Based on the Aztec calendar, this 1998 World Cup shirt knows what day it is.

### Cultural Leonesa

In 2014, the second division Spanish side donned suits and bow ties. Fancy!

### Chicago Red Stars

We award this team from the U.S. National Women's Soccer League four stars!

# STRIPE A POSE

A shirt with vertical stripes makes you look thinner and taller. A shirt with horizontal stripes makes you look shorter and wider. This optical illusion is one reason why vertical stripes are much more common than horizontal ones in soccer, but horizontal ones are more common in rugby. Soccer players like to look tall, while rugby players want to look as bulky as possible.

STAR STUDENT

JERRY C. STRIPES

❝ Look at me! ❞

STAR STUDENT **Stats**

Shirts in dresser: 580
Shorts in dresser: 400
Socks in dresser: 800
Washing machines: 10
Birthplace: Jersey City, New Jersey
Supports: Torns (Sweden)
Fave player: Jan Koller
Trick: Can turn defenders inside out

# FASHION QUIZ

1. **Which part of the soccer player's body was exposed during games for the first time at the beginning of the twentieth century?**

a) The neck
b) The belly button
c) The butt
d) The knees

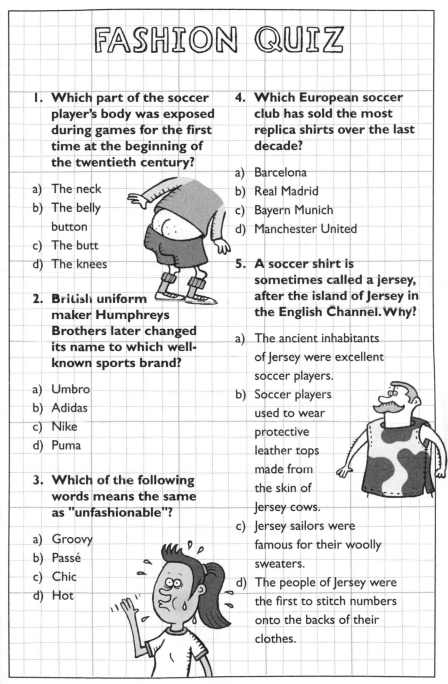

2. **British uniform maker Humphreys Brothers later changed its name to which well-known sports brand?**

a) Umbro
b) Adidas
c) Nike
d) Puma

3. **Which of the following words means the same as "unfashionable"?**

a) Groovy
b) Passé
c) Chic
d) Hot

4. **Which European soccer club has sold the most replica shirts over the last decade?**

a) Barcelona
b) Real Madrid
c) Bayern Munich
d) Manchester United

5. **A soccer shirt is sometimes called a jersey, after the island of Jersey in the English Channel. Why?**

a) The ancient inhabitants of Jersey were excellent soccer players.
b) Soccer players used to wear protective leather tops made from the skin of Jersey cows.
c) Jersey sailors were famous for their woolly sweaters.
d) The people of Jersey were the first to stitch numbers onto the backs of their clothes.

# ENGINEERING

It happens only a few times every year, and it's one of the most memorable, most photographed, and most symbolic sights in soccer: the moment when the team captain lifts the trophy to celebrate a victory.

In this lesson, we're going to ask why we use trophies to celebrate a win, and we'll learn about the materials they're made from. We will meet the oldest trophy in soccer and we'll hear about three trophy mysteries that have baffled the world.

Hands up if you're ready to lift the cup!

# LEAFY DOES IT

Your team has won the final. The glory is yours. Surely, that's all you need.

Not quite. It is human nature to also want a prize that you can look at and touch. This prize will be a constant reminder to you—and your rivals!—of your triumph. In nearly all sports, the winner of a tournament receives an object, known as a **trophy**, which reminds them of their moment of glory long after the event. Trophies are traditionally objects such as a cup, statuette, medal, or dish—or, in the case of Spanish bullfighting, one or two of the bull's ears. Oh, ear-ie me!

Trophies have been part of sporting events for thousands of years. In the ancient Olympic Games, the world's earliest major sporting tournament, dating from around 800 BCE, victorious athletes were crowned with a wreath of olive leaves cut from a sacred tree. Other Greek games gave crowns of celery leaves, pine leaves, or bay leaves. (Bay is also known as **laurel**, which is where the phrase "to rest on one's laurels" comes from, meaning to make no further effort because one has already achieved enough.)

Nowadays, trophies are usually made out of metal and, in the case of soccer, often shaped like a cup. Historians have long tried to get a handle (or two) on why a receptacle for drink became a symbol for sporting success, but the reason is not entirely clear. The first cups—wine goblets—began to appear as sporting trophies in the seventeenth century. By the time soccer became a popular sport, two hundred years later, the idea of cups as trophies was an established part of sporting culture. Up the cups!

## GOLD RUSH

The two most popular materials for trophies are gold and silver. These precious metals have long been associated with wealth. Here are some of the reasons gold and silver are considered valuable:

 They are both rare. You could fit every piece of gold ever mined in the world into a square box with 65-foot / 20-meter sides.

 They are lustrous. Most metals are gray or silvery gray, so gold and silver stand out and look pretty.

 They are long-lasting. More common metals tend to tarnish. When exposed to air and water, copper turns green and iron turns red, but gold and silver stay shiny for longer.

# SOFT TOUCH

Compared to other metals, gold and silver are both quite soft and **malleable**, meaning they easily bend. When gold or silver is used to make a trophy, the precious metal is usually mixed with other metals to make it harder and stronger. A material made from lots of metals is called an **alloy**.

The most common material used in making trophies is sterling silver, which is made of 92.5 percent pure silver. The remaining 7.5 percent is composed of other metals, mainly copper. Sterling silver is tough, and it's harder to scratch or damage than pure silver.

To make a gold trophy, pure gold is mixed with metals such as silver, copper, and zinc. Gold purity is measured using **carats**, a word that comes not from carrots but from the carob tree, whose seeds were used as weights when measuring out gold. Pure gold is 24 carats. The World Cup trophy is 18-carat gold, which means that it is 75 percent pure gold. That's enough gold to make it glisten, but it's tough enough to withstand a trophy celebration!

Because gold is so soft, it can be hammered into paper-thin sheets. Sometimes trophies are made of a material called **silver gilt**, which is silver covered with a thin layer of gold.

| TROPHY | | LOOKS LIKE | MATERIAL |
|--------|--|------------|----------|
| World Cup | | An ice-cream cone | 18-carat gold |
| Champions League | | Your aunt's favorite vase with winged handles | Sterling silver |
| Women's Champions League | | A plant with twisting vines | Sterling silver |
| Serie A | | A giant toothpaste tube with a funnel | Blue sodalite and silver gilt |
| Premier League | | A crown atop a vase with shield-style handles | Sterling silver |
| Bundesliga | | The fanciest fruit bowl ever | Sterling silver |
| Ligue 1 | | An old vinyl record with a soccer ball in the middle | Plexiglass, aluminum, and resin |

Ben and Alex's workshop

# A DAY IN THE LIFE OF SOCCER'S OLDEST TROPHY

The oldest soccer trophy in existence is the Scottish Football Association Challenge Cup. It has been presented to the winners of the Scottish FA Cup since the 1873–1874 season. With the help of the Scottish Football Museum's curator, the cup spoke exclusively to Soccer School.

I'm made of silver and almost 150 years old. I live in a glass cabinet at the Scottish Football Museum at Hampden Park stadium in Glasgow. I get scrubbed twice a year, and I've been cleaned so often that I've probably lost about half my original silver. It's an exciting life being the world's oldest soccer trophy!

I need to glisten on the day of the Scottish FA Cup final. It's my day of glory! Richard McBrearty, the museum curator, picks me up wearing white cotton gloves. I am guest of honor at a lunch for the two teams in the final. The guests gaze at me in awe. I look at them and pray they don't spill anything near me!

Richard moves me to an office and never takes his eyes off me during the game. True love! As soon as the final whistle blows, an engraver carves the winning team's name on a silver plaque on my plinth. (That's the wooden piece I stand on.) Then Richard whisks me off into the stadium!

I am handed to the captain of the winning team. By now, Richard is looking very anxious because he is no longer able to protect me. Chill out, Dickie! This is my moment! The stadium roars as the captain lifts me above his head. Then the team takes me onto the field for a lap of honor. Easy does it, boys! The players know to be careful—and the fans go wild when they see me!

When the team leaves the field, Richard is there. He gives them a replica cup, which looks just like me, and he is almost tearful with relief when he holds me again. Then I'm back in my cabinet, exhausted. What a magical afternoon!

# THE WORLD CUP TROPHY MYSTERIES

The original World Cup trophy, given to the winners of the World Cup from 1930 to 1970, has one of the most baffling histories in soccer. It was at the center of THREE separate mysteries and still to this day has not been found. Let's open the casebook to see if you can succeed where the world's best sleuths have failed.

DR. BELLOS
AND
SHERLOCK
LYTTLETON

# Mystery 1: The Rimet Riddle

FIFA president Jules Rimet asked Abel Lafleur, a sculptor from Paris, to design the trophy for the first World Cup competition, in 1930. Lafleur made a silver trophy of a cup being supported by Nike, the Greek goddess of victory, and coated it with gold. It was later renamed the Jules Rimet Trophy.

Experts believe something happened to the Jules Rimet trophy between 1954 and 1958. The trophy Brazil won in Sweden in 1958 looked different from the one that West Germany had won in 1954. The 1958 version appeared to be 2 inches/5 centimeters taller and had a different base.

```
MYSTERY: Was the 1958 trophy a
copy? If so, where is the original?
STATUS:
```

# Mystery 2: Stolen on a Sunday

In 1966, England hosted the World Cup. The Jules Rimet Trophy was on display in a central London museum for a few months before the tournament began. One Sunday, when the guards were not looking, a thief or thieves broke in through the back doors and stole the trophy. It was a huge embarrassment for English soccer, and Scotland Yard was called in to solve the crime.

```
MYSTERY: Where was the trophy?
STATUS: A dog named Pickles found
it seven days later wrapped in
newspaper under a bush
in South London.
```
SOLVED

```
MYSTERY: Who was behind the theft?
STATUS:
```
UNSOLVED

## Mystery 3: Burglary in Brazil

AU

FIFA had a rule that the first country to win the World Cup three times would be allowed to keep the trophy. When Brazil won their third title in 1970, the Brazilians took the Jules Rimet Trophy home. In 1983, it was stolen from the third floor of the Brazilian Football Confederation office in Rio de Janeiro. No one has seen it since. Brazil's investigators said that it had been melted down into gold bars, but this can't be right, since the original trophy wasn't made of gold!

```
MYSTERY: Where is the trophy?
STATUS:
```
UNSOLVED

After 1970, FIFA had a new trophy made. This one was made of gold and featured two human figures holding up a globe. So far this trophy hasn't gone missing. In fact, Ben once visited FIFA headquarters in Zurich and is one of the few Englishmen to have lifted it!

Whoever gets to the bottom of any of the three unsolved mysteries above would be a true world champion, a soccer Sherlock Holmes.

If you have any ideas, please let us know!

# CUP CALAMITIES

Defender Sergio Ramos dropped the Copa del Rey, or King's Cup, in 2011 when Real Madrid was parading through the city in an open-air bus. The bus ran over the cup and squashed it. Oops!

Fireworks and confetti were released as Brazilian team Corinthians lifted the trophy after winning the 2009 local championship. Some confetti and fireworks landed in the trophy and caught fire. Hot stuff!

The world's smallest soccer trophy is just ¼ inch / 6 millimeters high. It is given to the winners of the Lyonesse Cup, an annual match between the Isles of Scilly, which are just off Cornwall, and Dynamo Choughs, from Penzance. Not big but very Scilly!

Actual size

GOLDIE CUPP

☆ STAR STUDENT

66 Don't drop me! 99

☆☆☆ STAR STUDENT | Stats

Carat: 24
Carrots: 18
Carobs: 12
Ears: 2
Birthplace: The Gold Coast, Australia
Supports: Platinum Stars (South Africa)
Fave player: Lucy Bronze
Trick: Shiniest cleats in the world

# ENGINEERING QUIZ

1. **What was the prize for victorious athletes in the first Olympic Games?**

   a) A lifetime supply of olive oil
   b) A crown of olive leaves
   c) Shampoo made out of olive juice
   d) A golden olive

   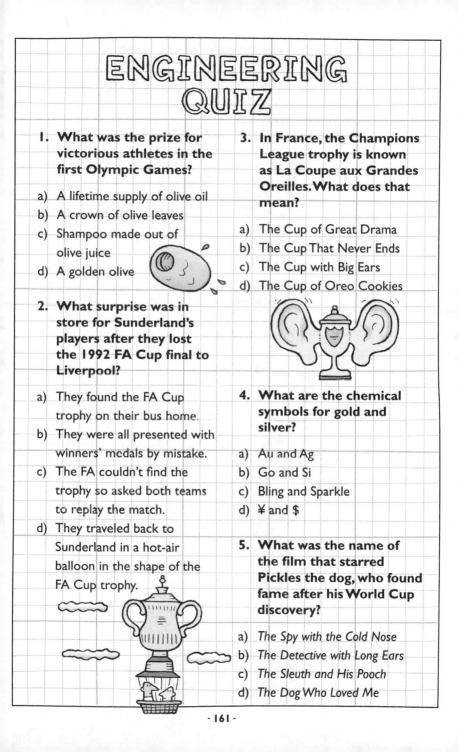

2. **What surprise was in store for Sunderland's players after they lost the 1992 FA Cup final to Liverpool?**

   a) They found the FA Cup trophy on their bus home.
   b) They were all presented with winners' medals by mistake.
   c) The FA couldn't find the trophy so asked both teams to replay the match.
   d) They traveled back to Sunderland in a hot-air balloon in the shape of the FA Cup trophy.

3. **In France, the Champions League trophy is known as La Coupe aux Grandes Oreilles. What does that mean?**

   a) The Cup of Great Drama
   b) The Cup That Never Ends
   c) The Cup with Big Ears
   d) The Cup of Oreo Cookies

4. **What are the chemical symbols for gold and silver?**

   a) Au and Ag
   b) Go and Si
   c) Bling and Sparkle
   d) ¥ and $

5. **What was the name of the film that starred Pickles the dog, who found fame after his World Cup discovery?**

   a) *The Spy with the Cold Nose*
   b) *The Detective with Long Ears*
   c) *The Sleuth and His Pooch*
   d) *The Dog Who Loved Me*

# QUIZ ANSWERS

**BIOLOGY**
1. a
2. c
3. b
4. d
5. c

**HEALTH**
1. c
2. b
3. c
4. d
5. c

**CHEMISTRY**
1. d
2. c
3. b
4. a
5. b

**ENGLISH**
1. b
2. c
3. c
4. a
5. a

**FIELD TRIP**
1. d
2. a
3. d
4. c
5. a

**FASHION**
1. d
2. a
3. b
4. d
5. c

**PHYSICS**
1. a
2. c
3. b
4. d
5. a

**HISTORY**
1. c
2. b
3. b
4. c
5. a

**ENGINEERING**
1. b
2. b
3. c
4. a
5. a

**ZOOLOGY**
1. d
2. a
3. a
4. b
5. d

**MATH**
1. b
2. a
3. c
4. b
5. d

**POLITICAL SCIENCE**
1. b
2. c
3. c
4. a
5. a

**GEOGRAPHY**
1. c
2. b
3. d
4. b
5. b

# ABOUT YOUR COACHES

**Alex Bellos** writes for the *Guardian*. He has written several best-selling popular-science books and created two mathematical coloring books. He loves puzzles.

**Ben Lyttleton** is a journalist, broadcaster, and soccer consultant. He has written books about how to score the perfect penalty and what we can learn from soccer's best managers.

**Spike Gerrell** grew up loving both playing soccer and drawing pictures. He now gets to draw for a living. At heart, though, he will always be a central midfielder.

## COLLECT THE SOCCER SCHOOL SERIES

# ACKNOWLEDGMENTS

We know that TEAM stands for Together Everyone Achieves More, and we are lucky to have the best team in the world at Soccer School. Once again, our illustrator, Spike Gerrell, has played a blinder. He wins the Soccer School Golden Crayon—thank you, Spike!

The backroom team at Walker has coached us to perfection. Head coach Daisy Jellicoe has led from the front, with great support from sporting director Denise Johnstone-Burt, along with Louise Jackson, Laurelie Bazin, Megan Middleton, Rosi Crawley, John Moore, Jill Kidson, James McParland, Ed Ripley, and Jo Humphreys-Davies.

We have loved working with our publicist, Jo Hardacre, and social media stars Naomi Bacon and Marion Honey.

Thanks to our agents, Rebecca Carter, Rebecca Folland, Kirsty Gordon, David Luxton, Rebecca Winfield, and Nick Waters, for keeping us fired up and focused.

We would also like to thank the following experts for sharing their time and knowledge with us: Simon Austin, Tony Barrett, Federico Bassahun, Michael Beale, Max Boon, Dr. Tony Collins, Dermot Corrigan, Andy Dixon, Reg Elliot, Dr. Luke Ettinger, Dr. Majid Ezzati, Tom Fattorini, Margaret Fern, Sarah Galgey, Ken Gibb, Serafino Ingardia, Hans Leitert, Nick Littlehales, Professor Stuart Lyon, Richard McBrearty, David McParland, Dr. Carmen Mangion, David Moor at www.historicalkits.co.uk, Matt Rapinet, Darren Rodman at Pitchmark Ltd., Nutan Shah and Ron McCulloch of the London Podiatry Centre, Luke Shiach, Dr. Stasinos Stavrianeas, and Adam Witchell.

Shout-out to our star students: Samuel Clegg, Ayalah Honigstein, Finn Inglethorpe, Matti Wilkins Strelitz, and Tami Wilkins Strelitz. And from Arnot St. Mary Primary School, Liverpool: Tamasin Robinson, Tom Kelly, and Emily Heavyside. From Knowsley Central School, Liverpool: Ava Dooley, Alfie Whittick, Ruby Wood, Todd Smith, Thomas Gibbons, and Tom Mather.

Ben would like to thank Annie for her continuing inspiration and support, and Clemmy and Bibi for adding the best jokes in here and cheering on Soccer School across the country.

Alex would like to thank Natalie for cheering from the terraces, and Barnaby and Zak for keeping the volume up.